the way of the cockroach

the way of the cockroach *Craig Hovey*

How Not to Be There When the Lights Come On and
Nine Other Lessons on How to Survive in Business

THOMAS DUNNE BOOKS
ST. MARTIN'S PRESS ⚮ NEW YORK

THOMAS DUNNE BOOKS
An imprint of St. Martin's Press

www.stmartins.com

Book design by Jonathan Bennett

Library of Congress Cataloging-in-Publication Data

Hovey, Craig, 1958–
    The way of the cockroach : how not to be there when the lights come on
and nine other lessons / Craig Hovey.—1st ed.
        p. cm.
    ISBN 0-312-34064-8
    EAN 78-0-312-34064-3
    1. Cockroaches—Fiction. 2. Success in business—Fiction. I. Title.

PS3608.O89W39 2005
813'.6—dc22
                                                                    2005048494

First Edition: January 2006

10 9 8 7 6 5 4 3 2 1

This book is dedicated to my friend, mentor, and teacher, Dr. John Charles Pool. Thanks for being at the right margin at the right time.

Acknowledgments

Many thanks to my editor at Thomas Dunne Books, Sean Desmond. In addition to vastly improving this book, he was a pleasure to work with from start to finish.

Thanks also to my grandparents, Reverend Harry and Elizabeth Goodrich. About fifty-five years ago they began digging, by hand, the foundation for what became a wonderful family cottage on Cape Cod. I finished writing the book there, and only wish it was good enough to capture the quality of their wonderful, loving spirits.

the way of the cockroach

you have nothing to fear but yourself

It wasn't 6 A.M. yet and Joseph was already toiling away at his desk, working to transform a tangle of dismal sales figures into a report that wouldn't get him fired when he presented it to Mr. Harshfeld after lunch. He pictured Harsh, as the boss liked to be called, sitting behind that big metal desk and shaking his head, frowning while he pretended to listen. His thick brow would bunch up and bear down over those flat cold eyes of his, eyes that were set too close together below a large wasteland of forehead that was steadily beating back his hairline.

The image made him shiver.

With only the light of a small desk lamp, and the sun just beginning to give the overcast sky a dull glow, his tiny universe, lit by a distant bank of windows, was dim. Little more than the shadows from other workspaces were visible beyond his cubicle.

Absently, Joseph reached into the top drawer of his desk and pulled out one of the awful nutrition bars his girlfriend, Monica, was convinced would help keep them healthy and regular deep into old age. Every bit of it was healthy, from the whole grains to the gummy fruit paste that held it all together. But the ingredients added up to the taste of used duct tape.

The break room was locked and he knew he had to eat. It was going to be another long, brutal day, so he would choke it down. He was so absorbed in trying to wish away the grim numbers before him that he did not look as he tore off the top of the wrapper and opened his mouth to take a bite.

Something fell into the pile of papers in front of him. It wasn't loud, but the noise was startling in the silent airplane hangar of a room. He leaned back a little and looked. It was a brown object, about a half-inch long, and, good god, it was alive!

A cockroach!

The disgusting thing had landed on its back and was wiggling its legs furiously in the effort to flip back over and get away. But it stuck in place. Joseph grabbed the printer manual from the computer stand to his right with both hands. Roaches scared him, and he was perfectly willing to sacrifice the paper it lay on in order to kill the foul thing.

Just as he raised the manual to nose level and prepared to deliver a death blow, he heard a small but clear voice.

"No, no, have mercy, please don't kill me, I beg you." Joseph looked around wildly. Somebody must have snuck in to play a trick on him. But all his coworkers were lazy slackers. Who among them had ever shown up at work, let alone gotten out of bed, this early? Again the voice came.

"Please, if there is a kind bone in your body, I've fallen and I can't get up. Don't kill me, I have kids—they need me!"

"Who's there?" Joseph shouted in his boldest voice. "I know you're around here somewhere. . . . You've had your fun, so come on out, I'm trying to get some work done here, for God's sake."

"I'm not having any fun at all, and I'm right here in front of you."

The voice came from the cockroach. Impossible! Somebody must have planted a fake bug on his desk and rigged up a tape player . . . but the legs were moving, and now he saw the antennae wiggling against the paper.

"Wow, I've got to start getting more sleep," he muttered to himself, "take a vacation, or take something . . . I'm hallucinating."

"No you're not. I'm real, and if you're not going to kill me, could you please help me get back on my feet? I promise I'll never bother you again, not ever."

Joseph looked back down at the cockroach. Its legs were moving slower now, just occasional spastic jerks, really, and the thing clearly wasn't going anywhere. He lifted the manual again.

"Whether or not you can really talk, I hate roaches. Time's up!"

"No, no." The legs began waving frantically again. "Don't kill me, I can help you, really. I know all about your problems here at work, and at home with Monica, too. I can help."

"What? You, a cockroach, know my girlfriend's name and can help me? This is too weird."

"It's true, and I know a lot more than that. For example, I know that you get only a small corner of the closet and that her toothgrinding keeps you awake at night, but you're afraid to tell her. I know about your wedding plans and where your honey-moon is going to be. Not only that but—"

"Hold on there, Mr. Cockroach," Joseph blurted out. "You can't know about my wedding because I'm not getting married, and even if I was, how in the world could you know anything about a honeymoon?"

"My name is Gregory, and I've been to your apartment plenty of times."

"What? But I live fifteen miles from here, that's impossible."

"No, it's really pretty easy, actually: I just hitch a ride in one of the empty pockets of your briefcase."

Joseph felt a wave of acid churn up in his empty stomach.

"That's awful. You mean to tell me I've been carrying roaches home? Monica would kill me if she knew."

"Don't worry, I'm the only one who's made the trip so far. That cucumber salad you brought into work was enough to keep any of my friends out."

"Hang on there, my mother gave me a big bowl of that a few months ago, after a family reunion—the stuff barely got touched. I brought some in for lunch one day."

"You sure did, in an old container that leaked all over the place. And you left it in there a week. Awful, just awful."

"What would a roach care about that? You'll eat anything."

"Not cucumbers. All of us hate cucumbers."

"Huh, who'd have guessed roaches were picky about any-thing?" Joseph remarked, then looked at the breakfast bar he'd dropped on the desk and suddenly felt faint. "Hey, what were you doing before you landed on my desk?"

"I was trying to eat breakfast."

"Breakfast?" Joseph moaned. "Now I'm really going to be sick."

"Oh, stop getting yourself all worked up over nothing. I was only nibbling on some of the glue used to seal the wrapper— on the outside."

"You sure you didn't get into any of my food?"

"No offense, Joseph, but those things don't look very appealing."

"You mean to say glue is better?"

"It sure is."

Joseph mulled this over for a few seconds.

"You're probably right."

"Now that you know I haven't contaminated your food, could you please help me get back on my feet?"

Not believing any of this, Joseph pulled a pencil from the desk's center drawer and laid it alongside Gregory, who immediately grabbed hold with the three feet on his left side and righted himself.

Gregory stretched while he said, "Thanks, that feels a lot better. Now, since you have spared me, which is a lot more than any of the bug-murderers you work with here would have done, I'm going to reward your kindness."

Joseph arched his still unbelieving eyebrows. "What are you going to do, give me a free room in a roach motel?"

"Nope. I'm going to tell you how to turn your life around."

Joseph just looked at him blankly for a few moments, then said, "Okay, you managed to sneak home with me a few times and you can talk, which, I admit, is pretty impressive for a roach, but I really doubt you have anything to share that's going to help me."

"Oh really? Listen, cockroaches were around 150 million years before the dinosaurs and 300 million years before your chimp ancestors figured out how to walk on two feet. We're the oldest insects that have survived to the present and, as the planet's senior and most adaptable six-leggers, we've always been on the cutting edge of evolution. Believe me, cockroaches know a lot more about how to survive and prosper anywhere, anytime, anyhow, than humans ever will. Why, if you knew what we know, you'd be running this whole company by now."

Joseph shook his head, amazed at the speech, and vaguely hoping the motion might clear away the sight of a talking cockroach on his desk.

"Did I really just hear a speech from a bug?" he mused to himself, with a combination of shock and awe.

Gregory waited in silence.

"Even if this is really happening," Joseph continued, giving in and addressing the bug, "what could you possibly tell me about running a company? You're just a glue-sniffing insect!"

"How little you know. For your information, Joseph, I am a member of *Supella longipalpa*, the brightest of all cockroach species—similar to Mensa in the human world. We've always preferred warm places, like libraries and appliances, and we have put our time spent in books and computers to good use."

"You mean that's where you learned to talk?"

"Bingo, my man, and we can write, too, but that is a little

more challenging. Now, let me prove myself by telling you how much I've picked up from your company phones and computers."

"Sure, I mean, what could be more normal than listening to a roach who spies on my coworkers?"

For the next ten minutes Joseph's eyes widened in amazement as Gregory filled him in on just how much he knew, describing the company and what it did in great detail and dishing out lots of juicy tidbits. The roach mapped out all the power struggles, the secret alliances, strategies to be unveiled in the months ahead, and even gave him the lowdown on a few office romances that left Joseph blushing. He leaned back and rubbed his chin.

"Maybe you really do have something to teach me; I guess it's good I didn't squash you after all."

"You got that right. There's an awful lot humans can learn from us. To prove it, since nobody else is here, well, no people anyway, I can start teaching you the Rules of the Roach."

"You can't be serious, the Rules of the Roach?"

Gregory ignored the remark and clambered up on Joseph's electric pencil sharpener and took a perch, looking like a professor getting ready to deliver a lecture.

"We tried to give the dinosaurs the same advice, but they didn't want to listen. I hope I have better luck with you."

Joseph was incredulous. "Cockroaches could talk to dinosaurs?"

"Sure, how can you survive if you can't understand what other creatures are talking about?" Gregory retorted, as though only members of an inferior race would be too lazy to match the accomplishment. Joseph briefly reflected back on his miserable performance in high-school Spanish. Bad enough that the roach knew so much more about his company than Joseph did, but a bug being just flat-out smarter than him was unthinkable. He had to resist.

"If you and your ancestors are so smart, how come it took you all those millions of years to come up with ten rules?"

Gregory moved his antennae in a way Joseph could swear was condescending. So now the thing was looking down on him? Great, a whole new bottom had been reached.

"The ten Rules of the Roach are just a shorthand way of summing up what we've learned through the ages. Are they simple? Of course—the greatest wisdom always is. And you shouldn't make fun of our rules until humans have survived for at least a few million years—long enough to prove yourselves."

"Whoa there, Mister Roach, you little creepy crawlers may have been around longer than us, but look at all we've accomplished. Name one thing roaches have done that compares with, oh . . . I don't know, the development of the Internet." And with that he puffed out his chest a bit and pointed at Gregory with his chin.

"That's easy," Gregory scoffed. "Humans have also created nuclear weapons, right?"

"Sure, what about it?"

"Now what would happen to you if a nuclear bomb were

planted beneath your desk and went off while you were in the middle of one of your little catnaps, or even a mile from here?"

Before he could stop the reflex, Joseph glanced into the murky recesses below his desk.

"I'd be dead of course. What's your point?"

"A cockroach can withstand about eighty times the radiation that would kill any human. Humans brag about the Internet, which is pretty impressive, but we took a huge evolutionary step forward that made us immune to the greatest human threat. Humans can blow themselves up and we'll go right on living, then outlive whatever comes along to take your place."

"Well, well, a cocky cockroach, huh? But even if you do have a point, what's that got to do with your rules?"

Gregory replied, "As you'll see, the Rules of the Roach are about the most important challenge facing every living thing, an issue to which humans pay far too little attention. How to survive anywhere, under any conditions, and continue to grow and evolve long after the larger, stronger, smarter creatures with greater resources have failed."

"Wait a minute, how can you say that? Humans are always struggling to survive. What do you think all our wars are about?"

"Your wars are about fear, which is the biggest threat to survival and success there is."

"How is fear a threat to survival? There are all kinds of things to be afraid of, especially today: There's terrorism, cancer—more frightening things than I could even count."

Gregory waited patiently while Joseph spoke, then replied,

"It isn't death or disease you need to be afraid of, but your own fear of them."

"Come again?"

"Getting scared over things you can't do anything about is silly. You end up creating all kinds of bogeymen you are terrified of, then chase yourself around with them. From there, anybody who convinces you they have control over what you fear becomes like a puppet master, one who can yank you around like a doll on a string."

"So what do you cockroaches do instead of getting scared? You mean to say, with all the things out there that can squash you, all the people who'd love to wipe out every last one of you, you aren't afraid?"

"What we do instead of living in a state of panic, like so many of you humans do, is keep our focus on what we can control."

"And what is that?"

"Our own business. For example, we can't do anything about humans building bombs, but we can work on dealing with reality—and that's why we're always the ones to survive."

Joseph heaved a huge sigh. "I can't believe it, I'm sitting here talking to a philosopher-king cockroach," he said, and shook his head to himself. "So nothing scares you, nothing at all?"

"No, there is one thing to be afraid of, to be very afraid of."

"Oh?" Joseph raised his eyebrows. "And what is this chink in the roach armor?"

"The only thing to fear is your own bad thinking. Nothing else can hurt you, ever."

"Look, you might be right, but this is too deep for me, and what good does it do me anyway?" Joseph swept his arm at the enormous room he was a speck in, like a game show host unveiling to a contestant a prize that had gone horribly wrong. "I'm stuck here in this prison."

Gregory did a full three-sixty pivot atop the pencil sharpener. "I see what you mean, but who put you here? Is this a sentence you have to serve?"

"Well, no, not exactly, but it's the best job I could find."

"Let me get this straight: Of your own free will you have accepted a position in 'prison' because you think it's the best you can do?"

"I don't know if I'd put it like that, exactly, but . . ." Joseph fumbled for words, "but I suppose . . ."

"Now do you see what I mean about having only yourself to fear? Who else could have done this to you?"

"Well . . ."

"Precisely. Look, let me give you the ten Rules of the Roach right now. They really can help."

"This I've got to hear."

"Actually, I already made a file of them on your computer."

"Impossible! That's impossible. How in the world can a roach type?"

"What I do is go to the basement and get the biggest of the American species of roaches living down there. Then I point out the right keys, one at a time, and my new friend climbs up to the top of your divider wall and jumps on them. It takes a while, but it works."

Joseph shook his head furiously, trying to clear the disturbing mental image.

"No way, it just can't be."

But a few minutes later, after he'd settled down enough to follow Gregory's instructions for retrieving the file, the rules flashed up on the screen:

THE TEN RULES OF THE ROACH

1) You have nothing to fear but yourself.

2) Don't always listen to your heart.

3) Always be the last bug standing.

4) Even the smallest opening can be a huge opportunity.

5) Feast where others see only garbage.

6) Grow eyes in your back.

7) Move while your enemies mull.

8) Rest up to wreak havoc.

9) Don't be there when the lights come on.

10) What doesn't exterminate you only makes you stronger.

That a roach could talk was more than enough new information for one morning. That a roach could operate a computer was seriously overloading Joseph's capacity to think. Slowly, through the fog of a mind ready to just pack it in, he read through the rules. It didn't help when, out of the corner of his eye, he saw Gregory put his roach-version of a chin in a roach-version of a hand—or at least a collection of hairs on the end of his right front leg—as he waited for Joseph to finish reading.

Joseph stopped halfway through the list and began to form a question, but suddenly Gregory vanished, as though he'd dissolved into thin air.

"Gregory?"

nasty bugs

"Gregory . . . Gregory . . . where did you go, you still here?"

Silence.

"C'mon out . . . Gregory?"

"Who are you talking to? There's no Gregory working here."

Joseph was badly startled by the voice behind him and swiveled in a panic to face the district manager, Mr. Lindley.

"G-G-Good morning, sir, I, ah, just came in early to get a jump on the day."

"It's not so early by my watch, why it's almost eight o'clock."

"Eight? That's impossible, it was six just a few minutes ago."

Mr. Lindley tipped his head back and let out a genial laugh.

"Well, I'd say we have a case of early-to-rise, quick-to-nap here, huh? Now really, you haven't been working all this time, have you, and what's that on your computer screen?"

With Mr. Lindley leaning closer and squinting at the screen, Joseph desperately stretched out his foot until he felt the surge protector under his desk and kicked the computer plug out of it.

"Whoops, the system crashed again," Joseph mumbled lamely. "Guess I'd better get it up and running again."

"Must have been a bug, right?"

"You've seen him, too?"

"What in the world are you talking about? Look," Mr. Lindley said, and put a comforting hand on Joseph's shoulder, "we've all peeked at naughty pictures."

"No, that's not it, Mr. Lindley, I'd never do that on company time, I'm . . ."

Lindley turned toward his office and waved Joseph off.

"Don't worry about it; I was young once, too."

To Joseph, Mr. Lindley seemed like a nice guy who somehow got by on very little visible work. The sales force was always beating the bushes for new deals; Harsh was always beating the sales force with new, higher quotas; but Lindley, the district manager and boss of Harsh and everybody else here in the Niagara Falls office, drifted in and out, seemingly untouched by the whole mess. His superior, a vice president whose name had never filtered down to Joseph's level, worked out of the company headquarters in Chicago, and Lindley traveled there a couple times a month.

Though everybody in Niagara Falls felt under the gun constantly, it didn't seem that anybody had Lindley lined up in their sights. Maybe he did more work than it seemed. He came from a wealthy New England clan and still summered at the family vacation home on Martha's Vineyard. Joseph had never "summered" anywhere.

Joseph wanted to protest his innocence some more, but Harshfeld's entrance made that a lost cause. As always, Harsh was outfitted in an expensive suit and tie that never quite fit him right. He was built like a beer keg and charged along on bowlegs, which reminded Joseph of a cartoon bulldog.

"Mornin', Mr. Lindley," Harsh said to his boss.

"Mornin', Joey. What we got going today?" he asked, turning to give Lindley his full attention and giving Joseph a view of his back.

"Well, I've got a bit of a hangover going," Lindley replied, "but nothing bad enough to keep me down. How about you?"

Harshfeld grinned, in fact, like a bulldog would if a bulldog could.

"Oh just a few beers at the rink after the game last night for me, nothin' serious. Maybe we need a little hair of the dog at lunch, huh Mr. Lindley?"

Lindley clapped Harsh on the shoulder and said, "First we better see what kind of business comes our way this morning."

"Certainly, certainly. How about we have Joey here go out and get us some doughnuts and coffee to help kick off the new week?" Harsh said, jabbing a blunt thumb over his shoulder in Joseph's direction.

"Now you're talking." And with that Mr. Lindley ushered Harsh toward his office. Quickly Harsh pulled a sweaty five-dollar bill, which looked like it had spent a whole season in one of his skates, from his front pants pocket, and tossed it on Joseph's desk without breaking stride.

In a show of resistance, Joseph didn't run right out the door to go fetch. Instead, he got up, stretched, and walked slowly to the men's room at the opposite end of the huge space, into which a steady stream of coworkers now trickled. He turned on the faucet, let the water run until it was ice cold, and splashed his face, then splashed it two more times.

Away from his desk he found it impossible to believe he had been talking to a cockroach. The whole episode must have been a dream, one of those that seem so real while you're in the middle of them, but then start fraying around the edges until you know they're not real. Lindley must really have woken him up; probably heard him talking in his sleep, too, which explained his mentioning Gregory. He'd better be careful. The last thing he needed was a reputation for talking to imaginary creatures.

Back in his cubicle everything looked normal. No sign of a talking roach. Joseph sat down with a sigh and shook his head ruefully. He picked up another page of dismal numbers and almost jumped out of his chair at the sight of Gregory there on the desk, chewing on a stray bit of Wite-Out.

"Man, this is good stuff. My grandfather was hooked on it back in the day, but you hardly ever see it in offices anymore."

"Well I suppose that's the price of progress," Joseph barely replied, the words almost choked off on account of his heart jumping into his throat.

"Yeah, there's a lot less bookbinding glue around now, too."

"Is that why some of my books at home are starting to fall apart?" Joseph asked suspiciously.

"I plead the fifth on that. Besides, this is even better. Just keep a bowl of it around and your books are safe, I promise."

"I can't take this," Joseph muttered, mostly to himself. Then he addressed Gregory. "On a more appetizing note, I need to make a trip for doughnuts and coffee, as you probably heard. Please do me a favor and don't be here when I get back, okay? No offense, but this just can't be happening."

Gregory hopped onto the pencil sharpener again and piped up, "Can I come, too? I take my kids there sometimes. No, no, not what you think," he added when Joseph started looking ill again. "We only go for the Dumpster, I promise."

"I'm not going to carry you, for God's sake; how are you going to come along?"

"The place is only a few doors down, I'll just crawl along the building walls."

Joseph shuddered at the vision, but didn't feel like arguing with a bug.

"Suit yourself."

As they made their way down the half block of office buildings, Joseph checked to make sure nobody was looking or listening when he addressed Gregory.

"You know, I never would have believed cockroaches had a whole philosophy of survival."

"Until a few hours ago you didn't think we could talk, either."

"The stuff you said about fear makes sense, the more I think about it, but can it really help me at work, with people like Harsh?"

"Look, Mr. Harshfeld is just as scared as you are. You need to remember that he isn't your problem, your own construction project is. You made him into a huge bogeyman, but if you look past the ugly mask you'll see that he is harmless, like an old, arthritic dog with no teeth and only a bark to intimidate people with. Once you drop this silly illusion, it will amaze you that he was ever an object of fear."

"How does that work?"

"Simple. He continues living in fear, tossed around by whatever master has control over the things he wants or is scared of. You, on the other hand, focus only on what is within your power to accomplish and stop worrying about the rest. You survive; you evolve. He fails."

"You mean like how the roaches kept going after the dinosaurs became extinct?"

"Yes, just like that."

"But survival is never a sure thing. Why, if somebody came along and smacked the wall you would be done for right now."

"So what? I'm a roach, not the god of all insects. I only live a little while, then it's time for me to make room for somebody else."

"Man, that sounds cold."

"Not at all. What's cold is to slam the window of opportunity on your own head and never go through it."

"Funny thing—now that you mention it, there aren't any windows in my work space." Joseph thought of the bare walls he spent his working hours trapped in. It occurred to him that the cubicle could easily be taken apart and reassembled somewhere else in minutes, with no record of him ever being within its confines.

"Then I guess you'll have to make your own windows, right?"

Gregory waited outside while Joseph went into the small bakery for coffee and doughnuts. They continued talking on the way back and Joseph forgot to make sure the coast was clear before entering the lobby of his building. He came to a stop behind a young woman already waiting for the elevator; she was new to the company and worked a couple rows of cubicles away from Joseph.

"You say something?" she asked, looking suspiciously over Joseph's shoulder.

"No, ma'am, I didn't."

"You weren't talking on a cell phone, or something?"

"No, not a thing."

After she resumed waiting for the elevator, Gregory inched up the wall and yelled out in his loudest voice, which the woman could barely hear.

"Hey, what's your number?"

She turned back around quickly, angry now, and asked Joseph, "You got a problem?"

Mortified, he flushed a deep red and began stammering, "No, no, I . . . I . . . uh . . . just have a bug and, ah, was sniffling, that's all."

She continued staring hard at him after he finished speaking, so Joseph decided it was a good day to take the stairs, fifth floor or not. Going up he was only briefly surprised to see Gregory keeping pace with him at eye level on the concrete wall.

"Well, I was definitely scared back there. I thought she was going to beat me with her shoe."

"No, that only would have happened if she saw me, but I am sorry about that. I just wanted to demonstrate how easy it is to spook you."

"Give me a break. Anybody would be spooked if a talking cockroach was out to get him in trouble. But you do have a point, sort of. I guess, to put it in your terms, I do need to grow a harder shell."

"Well put, but Joseph, you do not even *have* a shell. Right now you are like a dodo bird: a nice animal but completely defenseless—and not able to mount much of an offense, either."

"So what should I do? Is there hope for me, or am I doomed like a dodo?"

"You have plenty of potential, Joseph, we just need to start developing it. Why, you might just make a good roach after all."

"Thanks, I guess. So does this mean you're going to start teaching me those rules of the roach?"

"We've already begun."

"We have?"

"Yup, I've been giving you instruction in Rule Number One, just like it says on your computer: You Have Nothing To Fear But Yourself."

"Hey, you mean I'm already making progress? Alright!"

"Don't celebrate too soon. Rule Number One just sets the stage, the next nine call for hard work."

"What could be harder than learning to be fearless?"

"First of all, you've only heard about becoming fearless. You only really become that way after learning how to survive and prosper even when you have been squashed, decapitated, had your heart cut out, been poisoned, had to live with the curse of universal hatred—not to mention . . ."

"Hey now, hey now, you're not trying to scare me all over again, are you?" Joseph laughed.

"Not at all. If I wanted to do that I would have told you about the family reunion we just had in your cookie jar."

Joseph stopped dead in his tracks, horrified by a mental image of himself blindly reaching in for a handful of cookies, like he usually did a few times a day.

"Just kidding, bucko, you need to lighten up. Now let's get back to work."

the partner

Joseph groaned at the 7 A.M. alarm. True, he'd gotten up a lot earlier Monday, but after a long day of work and being knocked off kilter by his encounter with a talking cockroach, Joseph felt a powerful need for more sleep. He reached over to the night table and shut off the horrible foghorn-sounding device. It'd come into his life as a Christmas gift from Monica and he wished the stupid thing would break down or short out—anything that would silence it for good. No chance of that happening. Monica only bought the best. This was the Brink's truck of alarm clocks and not even a machine gun would stop it.

"Joseph, are you up?" Monica's voice cut through the haze he'd allowed himself to fall into.

"I am now, yeah."

"Could you come out here for a minute? I need to ask you about something."

He swung his legs over the side of the bed and almost fell flat on his face. For all the years between graduating from college and moving in with Monica Primson four months ago, he'd lived in apartments where his mattress sat on top of a box spring, a simple arrangement to get in and out of. Now, though, he shared a bed that was propped up by a huge metal frame, and the height it added meant his feet dangled six inches over the floor when he sat on the edge. He still hadn't gotten the hang of it. Many a day began with him flailing out of the bedroom like he'd run down a flight of stairs and missed the last step.

Joseph stumbled to the bathroom and threw cold water on his face and toweled off. He avoided eye contact with the haggard face in the mirror and walked out to the spacious living room.

Monica, having commandeered the good space by the bank of windows for her morning routine long before Joseph moved in, strode along at a rapid clip on her treadmill. In front of her the television was tuned to CNN. At her left was a raised coffee table with three newspapers, four magazines, and two books arranged on it. With a coordination Joseph would never attempt, Monica could scan through all of them without breaking stride or missing anything important on the news.

On a matching table to her right was a large covered plastic cup that she drank a fruit smoothie from with a straw, and beside that another of the never-ending variety of nutrition bars she bought at the health food store near her office. It looked like a beat-up wallet.

Monica never set the treadmill at an incline, even though she could easily handle it. She feared developing too-bulky muscles that wouldn't flatter an on-the-move personal injury attorney who wanted to look feminine in court—and in the office. Under her father's watchful eye, Monica was scrambling up the ladder at the law firm he was the managing partner of.

In college, Monica was among the best on the woman's crew team. Born with a sturdy frame that grew to six feet, the rowing gave her a powerful physique. Joseph had seen the pictures of her from back then, aglow and happy with the team, a beauty in her element. The last time he tried to tell her that she'd dismissed him.

Joseph walked over to the refrigerator for some orange juice and poured a glass, drinking it where he stood at the counter that separated their small kitchen from the living room. Monica looked at him from the opposite side of the room.

"Are you still planning on taking me to your company's Spring Fling in the Park this Saturday? Dad's firm was invited, too, since we do all your legal work, and everybody will be there, all the partners and their wives."

Having forgotten all about it, he stalled. "Oh, I didn't know your firm allowed us wives to tag along."

"Now don't get your shorts in a twist," she admonished him in a courtroom voice. "These kinds of events are more important than you realize."

"I'm not sure if I can make it. Harsh said something yesterday about how I might have to go out of town Friday and Saturday, some sort of company sales meeting on a new product they've got coming out."

"Oh please," Monica scoffed. "What kind of new product does a plumbing supply company need to talk about, a heated toilet seat?"

"Now, Monica, you're the one always telling me I've got to get out there and shake more trees to grow my commissions— or maybe shake more handles is a better way to put it." He grinned at his joke, an appreciation she didn't share.

Monica did something Joseph had never witnessed her do: She stopped the treadmill before the timer went off. This must be serious, he thought. She stepped off the machine and gave Joseph an irritated look.

"You're going to let that awful man send you off to God-knows-where on such short notice, on another weekend? We had plans, you made a commitment to me. I can't just go by myself, it'd look terrible."

Joseph was getting used to Monica's temper, which erupted often enough that it was already part of their routine, but she looked upset now and the tremble in her voice made him uncomfortable.

"Look, Monica, I'll check with Harsh today, okay? He didn't say I had to go anywhere for sure, so maybe there's nothing to be worried about."

"You'll talk to him first thing?"

"Yes, I promise."

"Okay." She nodded her head decisively and turned the machine back on and remounted it.

"I'll give you a call at ten o'clock this morning to see how it went."

"Great, just what I need," Joseph muttered to himself.

"What was that?"

"I said I hope they put your call through with all due speed."

Their apartment was situated on the edge of a three-block section that sported the city of Buffalo's only upscale urban life past five o'clock in the evening. Neither Monica nor Joseph participated in much of it, at least not since he'd moved in with her.

Joseph had met her early the previous fall in a shimmering martini bar called Chrysler's, which had closed by the time Joseph moved into Monica's apartment the first week in December. It was the bar's Saturday Night Networking event that brought them together. The gimmick worked by having women put their business cards in one hat, with men dropping theirs into another. Five cards were randomly pulled from each and the lucky couples were matched up and treated to free jumbo martinis in a large, semiprivate booth in back.

When Thanksgiving rolled around, Joseph discovered that they were a committed couple. Official notification that the deal had been scaled came in the form of an invitation to appear with her for Thanksgiving dinner at her parents' Amherst estate. Monica's parents hadn't exactly showered him with affection, and somehow made it clear, without saying so, that Joseph was only there because nobody more suitable had stepped forward yet.

No matter what the weather, Monica power-walked the two miles to her father's law firm every morning in a pair of lightweight running shoes that got traded in for heels in her office, a selection of which took up most of the coat closet. Joseph said she was out to become the Imelda Marcos of ambulance chasers. To her credit she saw some humor in that, but it didn't slow down the ongoing shoe-shopping spree.

Work for Joseph meant a trek to downtown Niagara Falls, where his company leased a crumbling old building as their regional headquarters. Three floors were devoted to inventory storage and two more housed the administrative, sales, and marketing functions. About half his time was spent on the road, which meant a dreary succession of one-star hotels where the television remotes were bolted to furniture. It seemed that the company was determined, no matter how far he traveled, to find him rooms in places on par with the 70's style, one-floor motels that dotted Niagara Falls Boulevard, where the morning towels smelled like last year's cigarette smoke.

Once he was showered and dressed, Joseph gave Monica a peck on the cheek, careful not to incur her wrath by smudging the makeup that was now sculpted in place, filled a travel mug with the last of the coffee, and headed out to his car. It was a beautiful spring morning, the kind that makes Buffalo residents feel like falling to their knees and thanking whatever weather gods had decided to finally give them a break. Joseph's mood was elevated so much he whistled a happy tune all the way to his car.

He slid behind the wheel, threw back a big mouthful of coffee, and set his cup securely in the holder between the front seats. His compact car's engine never seemed to Joseph to be much more powerful than the one on his father's old riding lawnmower, but it came to life like clockwork. In reverse now and checking for traffic before backing out of his parking spot,

Joseph switched the defroster on high to quickly clear away the thin layer of morning frost on his windshield.

Suddenly a gray object with wings shot out of the vent and took hold on the inside of his windshield. But only for a fraction of a second, before being forced upward another few inches, where, using its four wings to brake like a dragster parachuting past the finish line, it gained a foothold.

Joseph gagged on his coffee and went into a coughing fit, which painted the glass in front of him a light brown. Once he gained control of himself he looked and saw that, somehow, the thing had dodged all the coffee and was now perched on the dashboard, watching him.

It was Gregory!

"My God," Joseph croaked. "How'd you get in here?"

"Whew, that was a wild ride. I was up there sunning myself and fell asleep on a dust ball. I woke up when you opened the door, but was disoriented and fell into the air vent, and the rest, as you humans say, is history."

"I didn't know you could fly."

"I can't, much. I hardly ever use my wings," Gregory said, and gave them a brief flutter to demonstrate, "but they did help slow me down enough so I didn't get blown away."

Joseph slumped back into the seat and looked at the mess in front of him.

"Oh no, how am I going to get this cleaned up before work?"

"Look, it's not that bad; none got on your clothes, and, since you take a lot of sugar in your coffee," and here Gregory paused to lap up a sample, "I'm sure I could round up a few friends who would make the inside of your car look like new."

"Oh that's great, a cleaning by infestation. I should open a business with that name."

"I'll provide the employees—and they all work for free."

"Real funny. How about I just go inside and get a roll of paper towels?"

"A waste of good coffee, but suit yourself."

Five minutes later Joseph returned with a roll of paper towels and a bottle of spray cleaner. Monica, with her hair pulled back and tied tight, looking stern and impatient, was at his heels.

"How in the world did you get coffee on the inside of the windshield?" she asked him, after peering inside.

"I got some caught in my throat, I guess."

"Coffee, a fluid, caught in your throat?"

"Well then, it must have gone down wrong. It'll just take a second to clean up. You want a ride to the office?"

"And pull up in this?" Monica motioned at the early 90's compact. "The cleaning ladies get dropped off in better cars. Besides, it's nice out and I need to get my walking in, which, by the way, wouldn't be a bad idea for you. You could stand to tighten up your middle a bit."

Joseph glanced at his stomach self-consciously.

"What, and walk all the way out to Niagara Falls Boulevard? It'd take all day."

"Then why not go in early and walk down to the Falls? There are some nice paths to walk on in the park."

"Good idea, maybe I'll do that," Joseph replied, not wanting to be rude by starting to wipe up the coffee while Monica spoke, but antsy to get going.

"I doubt it. Anyway, I've got to get moving—I'll call at ten," and with that she turned her purposeful stride toward the sidewalk.

Cruising down the boulevard, Joseph kept glancing over at Gregory, who sat in the passenger seat. He was still not ready to completely give up hope that the new day had dawned free of talking cockroaches.

"Your Monica is quite a woman," Gregory observed.

"Yeah, she's something else alright."

"She reminds me of an insect that's almost as highly evolved as us roaches; a predator of ours, in fact."

"On bad days she reminds me more of a bull in a china shop than any kind of insect I can think of."

"Oh no," Gregory corrected him, "Monica is clearly evolving into a queen bee."

"Come again?" Joseph said, turning his head to peer at Gregory while they were stopped at a light.

"In a bee colony, prospective queens are identified early on and anointed with jelly from the workers, which gradually turns them into queens."

"Is that what's happening in her father's law firm?"

"A human version, yes, and do you know what that makes you?"

"Do I want to know?" Joseph asked, his eyes back on the road again as traffic surged ahead.

"A drone."

"Aren't those the bees that only exist to impregnate the queen?"

"You got it, and now you know why those secret wedding plans exist."

"But that doesn't make any sense. Don't I have to know about my own wedding; when was she planning on telling me?"

"When you were a little further along in your dronehood and unlikely to argue about it."

"What kind of a relationship is that?"

"A queen bee's relationship, Joseph; they aren't big on sharing power. For example, there can only be one queen in a hive, and if there is more than one they'll fight to the death, or one or more of the queens might fly off to a new colony that needs them."

"And queens fighting has what to do with me?"

"To go back to Rule of the Roach Number One, Monica is evolving into a very powerful woman and you are living in her hive. You can leave, negotiate a better position for yourself, or simply accept being a drone—which is the path you are on now."

Joseph's voice rose indignantly. "I'm not going to allow any woman to do that to me!"

"Calm down, tiger. There's much to admire in powerful queens. She's not doing anything to you, it is you, in being fearful of her, who leads you to dronehood."

"Okay, I've got a question for you, since we talked about Harsh yesterday and Monica today. Which one is toughter?"

"That's easy. She'd eat him alive."

"I'm doomed," Joseph groaned.

don't always listen to your heart

Joseph managed to make it to work on time, but it was the worst kind of morning. He spent it making cold calls to builders, wholesalers, and retailers in the effort to set up appointments. Having been there long enough to know the math, Joseph understood that it took an average of three dozen calls to people who generally didn't want to hear from him to set up one appointment, and of the appointments he set, one in fifteen, if he was lucky, would result in an order being placed.

For a national company, the regional sales force stationed in Niagara Falls to serve the northeastern United States and Canada was small, so Harsh had plenty of time to devote to each of them. His brainstorm of a few months ago had been to install counters on the phones that kept track of the amount of calls made, how long they lasted, and the numbers they went to—just like his buddies who worked the penny stock boiler rooms down in Boca Raton did.

He'd sit behind his desk with the call screen in front of him and keep close tabs on the six salespeople stationed in their cubicles. Any sign of slacking off brought him rampaging out of his office, and no excuses were accepted. With only a modest base salary and the rest of his earnings determined by their performance, which was the one thing Lindley seemed to have a clear handle on, he was strongly motivated to drive them as hard as he could. Plus, it was fun.

Joseph had put off asking Harsh about the possible weekend trip, but now it was 9:45 A.M. and he needed to have something to report to Monica. If he lied—and he was mystified by how she always knew—she'd only berate him until the fib was exposed. Better to face up to Harsh.

"Excuse me, Mr. Harshfeld?" Joseph intoned meekly, having stuck his head out of his cubicle when he heard Harsh come barreling past.

"What's up, Joey, can't you see I'm in a hurry?"

It was hard to form words with Harsh looming over him with his arms crossed over his broad chest, but Joseph managed.

"I was just wondering, do you know if I'm going to have to travel this weekend?"

"Oh, you mean for that meeting we've got going?"

"Yes, I believe so."

"What day is it today, Joey?"

"Tuesday, Mr. Harshfeld."

"Okay, and when would you leave?"

"Probably Friday morning," he replied, knowing that unless the site was extraordinarily far away Harsh would insist he leave early rather than allocate department funds for two nights in a hotel room.

"So I'll let you know Thursday afternoon. Anything else you need?"

"Not that I can think of, no."

"Then get back to work," Harsh commanded, and strode off to his office and his beloved counting machine.

"Hey, Joseph, how's it going?" came a much more appealing voice at a couple of minutes before ten, which had an immediate soothing effect on both the lingering sting from his interaction with Harsh and the dread of Monica's call.

"Good morning, Karen," he replied, trying to keep his voice steady even as he felt his chest constrict, as it did every time he saw her. "What's up?"

Karen had long dark hair that she wore loose today. It flowed nearly all the way down her back and looked great with the gray cashmere sweater, jeans, and boots she wore. She always dressed well, but never to show off and always simply, and light on the makeup. And there was a natural lack of self-consciousness in her look that amplified how pretty she was.

"Nothing much," she answered, "just trying to get the next set of ads out on time is all."

"Man, you marketing people have it great; nobody yelling at you, you get to be creative . . . have real offices."

She shrugged where she stood, with one shoulder leaning against the entrance to his closet-sized cubicle.

"It's not bad, but the second our stuff stops working we're gone, and we know it."

"And that doesn't bother you?"

"Why should it? This isn't exactly Madison Avenue we're

talking here. Hey, a few of us are heading over to Alcorn's for lunch, you want to come?"

He felt like a light switch had just been turned on inside him.

"Sure, of course, that is, if you don't mind."

"Mind?" Her brow furrowed a bit, which only made her more attractive. "Didn't I just invite you?"

"I guess you did, how about . . ."

Joseph was cut off by the telephone, and his heart sank when he saw the number displayed.

Monica.

Seeming to understand what he was in for, Karen said, "Look, we'll meet up downstairs at noon, okay?"

Joseph nodded in agreement and picked up the phone.

"Joseph?"

"Hi, Monica, how's your morning going?"

"Fine. Did you speak to Harshfeld?"

"I sure did. I told him it wasn't fair to send me off again without more advance notice, and that I already had plans, so we agreed that he'll only send me if there's absolutely nobody else who can go."

"Really?" she asked suspiciously.

"The truth, I swear."

"It better be, because . . ."

Joseph got through the rest of the conversation on autopilot, and stayed in that mode until it was time for lunch.

Alcorn's was a pub just a couple miles away that had recently become popular with Joseph's coworkers, though he hadn't been there yet. Karen's offer to drive came as a relief, what with his fears of having missed a coffee splash or two in his haste to clean up earlier, and he got a kick out of her car, a late-60's Mustang she had restored herself, though hardly any of the guys in the office believed it. Joseph had asked her enough about it to know her passion was genuine and she spent many a weekend in her garage doing every speck of work possible on it by herself.

Being with Karen was exciting. Not just because she was pretty, but because she was smart, funny, and vibrant, too—and Monica would kill him if she found out. In her mind, "just lunch" would not equal innocence. They were led to a table big enough for eight, but nobody else was there yet.

"Did the others decide not to come?" he asked, with hope springing in his heart.

"Oh I'm sure a few will show up; it's pretty casual. You want to look at a menu?"

Over the next few minutes three more of their coworkers did show up, which wasn't ideal in Joseph's mind, but they were female friends of Karen's, which helped. That changed when he looked outside and saw a bright red, late 90's Dodge Intrepid with oversize tires pull up outside.

A chunky, medium-height man about Joseph's age emerged. He wore pleated slacks and a knit sweater with a v-neck that plunged into a thick tangle of dark chest hair. He straightened his head and whipped his long bangs out of his eyes with a devil-may-care gesture he would repeat every three minutes. It was

Gerald Smith, the self-proclaimed company lady's man and self-appointed heir to Harshfeld's throne.

"You invited him?" Joseph asked, hoping to hear Smith had shown up to meet another party.

"Sure, why not?" one of the girls said. "He's fun."

Karen rolled her eyes at Joseph and he felt better about it—until Smith waltzed over to the table, kissed all the girls lightly on the tops of their heads, gave Joseph the briefest of nods, and sat down on the other side of Karen. To make matters worse, he started talking cars, which captured Karen's attention and left Joseph out in the cold, afraid to join a conversation where his ignorance would quickly embarrass him. Just his luck, Smith seemed to know enough about the trials and tribulations of keeping a vintage car going to hold Karen's attention.

Smith had started working in sales a few months after Joseph's arrival. For some reason, though his and Joseph's numbers were always pretty close, Smith was able to avoid Harsh's wrath and had even weaseled his way into becoming a sort of mascot for the men's league hockey team Harsh was so proud of playing on. Smith rarely got stuck with the bad weekend sales trips unless, of course, it was somewhere he wanted to visit, and somehow he managed to stay in better hotels and eat in better restaurants than Joseph.

After a while Smith abandoned car-talk in favor of regaling

the table with inside company gossip nobody was supposed to know about, but, if they all promised to keep it to themselves, what could it hurt? He liked making fun of Harsh and Lindley behind their backs, too, and told tales of how he stood up to the both of them when he needed to, a feat unequaled in company lore.

Worse than all the garbage Smith shoveled out was noticing that Karen seemed to become increasingly interested in him as the lunch hour progressed. Now Joseph was miserable and wished to God he had never agreed to come.

On the way back to the office Joseph sat silently and pouted as Karen drove.

"Hey there, you, is something wrong? You look down in the dumps."

"It's just that Smith; he's so full of it."

Karen chuckled. "That's what's bugging you? He's not a bad guy, as far as I can tell, and he does know his classic cars."

"I hope one runs him over," Joseph muttered darkly.

"What was that? I didn't hear you."

"Nothing, but you know, the way he talks about work you'd think the company was going to make him king."

"He has been the top salesman for the last few months, hasn't he?" Karen asked, and then realized her mistake. "Except I know you are right on his heels."

Joseph didn't even bother to correct this, and just stared out the window for the rest of the ride.

Much later in the day, after all the surrounding cubicles had emptied out and Joseph was getting ready to do the same, Gregory appeared on the lip of his desk.

"How did lunch go with Karen today?"

"I don't want to talk about it."

"That's what I thought, you've looked pretty glum ever since you came back. Are you still just flirting with her or have you gotten more ambitious?"

Indignantly, Joseph straightened his tie and sat up stiffly.

"Despite our earlier conversation about bees and such, you know I'm committed to Monica. What's the matter with you?"

"Me? Nothing. I've got five thousand kids and grandkids with the same woman and have never strayed. You're out for a change before you produce even a single brood—pretty fickle I'd say."

"Look, Gregory, I'll level with you. Karen does something for me that hasn't happened before. It just seems like we're perfect for each other, but you are a bug, after all, and there's no way you can know what the human heart is like."

"I do know one very important thing."

"And what's that?"

"Rule of the Roach Number Two: Don't Always Listen to Your Heart."

"That's insane. You mean to tell me you don't believe in love, in finding your soul mate?"

"I didn't say that. Remember, the rule says not to always listen to your heart—it doesn't say never listen to it. But the problem is, what you humans mistake for the murmurings of your hearts is usually nothing more than chemical reactions that have been reinforced by millions of years worth of evolution."

"If you think that explains how I feel right now, you're nuts."

"No, you're nuts at the moment, and you've been made that way by a special kind of perfume."

"You mean Karen has some kind of special potion she uses to get me feeling this way? That's even wackier."

"Exactly, though she probably doesn't know it. In cockroaches and lots of other insects this special perfume is called pheromones. Females give it off when they are ready for courtship and reproducing. It gets into the air and males who get a whiff come running, just like they are programmed to."

"But that's for bugs! Humans can think and make decisions," Joseph replied, but then remembered how Smith made his way to their table so quickly at lunch.

"Oh? Not when it comes to the laws of attraction. Humans respond to similar chemicals, they just haven't been around long enough to discover them, like we have. Karen, for example, is a human pheromone factory. You think you are the only one to come sniffing around?"

"Well, she hasn't said anything about being involved with anybody. Hey, but if pheromones do this, why don't I feel the same way for Monica?"

"You did, a few months ago, but now that she feels your relationship is stable—little does she know, yet—her body does not produce as much of that special perfume."

Joseph thought back to the night he met Monica and how

strongly he was attracted to her. She was tipsy, though not drunk, and having a blast downing martinis with her friends—coworkers from the public defender's office. On a dare she'd asked Joseph to dance and they ended up drinking and dancing together until closing time, then went out to breakfast and talked until midmorning.

She'd gone to work at the public defender's office, against the wishes of her father, straight from law school and stayed for five years. Gradually, dad wore her down. First, it was just moonlighting for him to supplement her meager public defender's salary, then sneaking in some sick days to help out with demanding cases.

Then, all of a sudden, the firm's business took off as the result of a steady barrage of television advertisements seeking clients who'd experienced negative side effects from drugs, everything from Viagra to cholesterol medications. What seemed to do it was their "Long Arm of the Law" theme, which showed evildoers being grabbed by a huge hand, turned upside down, and shaken until money flew out of their pockets.

Monica was reborn as a personal injury attorney.

That first night at the bar was the one and only time Joseph had seen Monica tipsy. After Thanksgiving she went to work for dad, and what Gregory had identified as an anointing-by-jelly began turning her into a queen of the courtroom.

"Am I really that chemically shallow?" Joseph asked.

"Sure, you and most males everywhere, of every species. Where humans are different is that since they can think and talk, they confuse biology with some kind of grand passion. What you need to do instead is let your gift of reason take over. Observe, think things through, don't be misled by a reflex that leads you into a trap."

"Maybe Monica's more like a spider, then, luring me into her web?"

"No, she's definitely a queen bee well along in her training. Queen bees use pheromones, too, and give their drones and workers instructions with them."

"But if I'm not feeling them anymore, why am I still attached to her?"

"She does still give them off once in a while, just like any good queen. If the pheromone payoff completely stopped, you'd look elsewhere, but if you still think it'll arrive occasionally, but can't predict when, you can end up waiting a long time."

"So Monica really has me bamboozled, huh?"

"No, you bamboozle yourself, but she has a strong instinct for helping the process along."

In thinking this through, Joseph had to admit, reluctantly, that Gregory had some real insight into where he was at, though he wasn't ready to admit it.

"I don't know, your ideas are going to take some getting used to," he said.

"While you're getting used to them, bear in mind that people respond to all kinds of signals from each other, like sights, smells, and postures. At work, as in love, it is easy to go with what you think is a heartfelt emotion, only to make a bad decision because you let an ancient reflex dictate policy in a new and completely different environment."

"So that's why you shouldn't always listen to your heart?"

"Not so that you make decisions with it. Ancient instincts are fine for ancient species; humans just get in trouble with them."

flower power

Already it was three-thirty and Harsh hadn't said a word to him about the weekend yet. At noon Joseph had stopped answering Monica's calls which, between his cell and office lines, added up to a staggering assault. More frightening yet was anticipating her reaction if he arrived home without an excuse. On one hand, going away for a couple days right now, even if it was to a lame sales meeting with a bunch of dozing, overweight guys with bad, or fake, hair, would give him a much-needed break from Monica. On the other hand, though, she'd be so angry he'd be sure to pay a steep price for the days off. He sighed heavily and laid his forehead on the desk.

"Sit up and grab the phone, fast, the boss man is coming," said an urgent voice.

Dazed and confused, Joseph jolted upright, hit himself in the side of the head with the receiver, and began dialing blindly.

"Well, about time," said Harsh, as he filled the space between the dividers. "Your call count has been sinking like a rock today."

"Yes sir, Mr. Fisk, I'll be happy to check and see if we have enough in stock to fill your order, then I'll get back to you.

Thank you, sir," Joseph said politely, and hung up the phone. "Sorry, Mr. Harshfeld, I didn't hear you."

"Hummphh," the scowling man grunted. "Hey, look here, Joey, the company lawyers told us to cancel that sales shinding over the weekend, something about how there's a hang-up getting the patent in order, or some such, so you don't have to go."

"Thank you so much for telling me, Mr. Harshfeld," Joseph replied, with more sarcasm than he'd aimed for.

"You getting smart with me?"

"Not at all, no, I'm just glad for the chance to be here tomorrow, that's all; it'll give me a chance to catch up on some paperwork."

"Is that so? Speaking of catching, I put you down for playing in the company softball game at the picnic Saturday. You got a mitt?"

"Sure, or I think I still do. I'll be glad to be a part of your team, Mr. Harshfeld."

"My team?" Harsh responded, and laughed enough so that his belly rose and fell a couple times. "You're not playing on my team, I want to win."

He started to walk away, then snapped his fingers and came back.

"Joey, I almost forgot, I need to go over a couple accounts with you—I know we can squeeze more out of these guys."

As Harsh began his usual grilling, and Joseph supplied his usual answers, Joseph noticed that Gregory had walked up the divider wall and climbed on top of a thumbtack stuck to it. As Harsh spoke, Gregory began imitating him. Somehow the roach managed to affect a beer belly and Harsh's wide-footed stance, and began moving his mouth and antennae in a perfectly coordinated parody of Harsh's speaking style and gestures. It was all Joseph could do to stifle a laugh.

"What's so funny, huh, Joey? You think leaving dollars on the table is a good thing for the company, is that it?"

"No, no, not at all," he replied, for the first time not feeling frightened by Harsh.

"You realize, don't you, that lost dollars for the company means less dollars in your pocket, you realize that?"

Gregory let his antennae drop and lowered his head in an uncanny reflection of Harsh's glower. Joseph had to put his hand over his mouth and turn away. Lucky for him, the phone rang at that moment.

"Hello?"

Behind him Joseph heard Harsh hiss, "Hello? That's not how you're supposed to answer the phone and you know it. . . ." The rest was drowned out in Joseph's ear by Monica.

"Just why in hell haven't you returned a single one of my calls?"

"Yes, ma'am, in fact, we carry a full line of the very best in elite faucet fixtures. Has your store ordered from us in the past? Oh, you have? Yes, Gerald Smith is still with us, would you like to speak with him? No? I'm sorry to hear he acted that way toward you. Please accept my assurance that I will treat you with the utmost respect."

Joseph continued on in this vein until Harsh lost interest and stalked off, then he switched to his civilian voice.

"Hi, Monica, how's it going?"

"What was that all about?"

"Oh, just joking around with some of the guys, no big deal."

"It's a big deal if you do it on my time, mister. Look, are we going to the picnic together or not?"

"Yes, we are," he replied, then lowered his voice to continue. "I finally had it out with Harshfeld. I told him he didn't let me know soon enough and that I wasn't willing to disrupt another weekend."

"Well good for you, it's about time. You're finally growing a spine."

"Is that as good as a shell?" he asked, eying Gregory, who was still on the thumbtack, as he spoke.

"A shell? Have you lost your mind?"

"No, no, I'm sorry. But look, isn't that great, we can go to the picnic together."

"It is certainly a relief to have that settled. What time will you be home from work?"

"Probably around six or so."

"Fine. Could you pick something up for dinner at Tang's, maybe some brown rice and steamed vegetables? I won't be home until eight."

"Sure, sweetheart, I'll see you then."

"See you." The phone went dead.

Joseph set the phone down and shook his head ruefully.

"The bloom's off the rose?" Gregory asked, having climbed back down the divider and up on the pencil sharpener.

"Maybe. I have a feeling those phera-whatevers aren't coming back any time soon."

"It's been my experience that having a break from them is not a bad thing; it gives you some breathing room."

"Breathing room for what?"

"For clear thinking on whether what you are involved in is right for you or not."

"But what about Karen? I feel just as strongly for her as I did for Monica. But if it's all chemicals and instincts, aren't I just setting myself up for another set of problems? Listen to me, here I am worrying about a relationship with Karen when I doubt she's even interested."

Gregory moved toward Joseph, as though to comfort him.

"Don't forget, sometimes your heart is right."

By the time he left, Joseph was among the last remaining workers. Lindley and Harsh had split shortly after his conversation with Monica, and that's all it took for the early exodus to begin. Approaching his car, Joseph felt a tingling race up and down his spine when he spotted Karen's Mustang a mere three spaces away. He slowed his pace and looked furtively over his shoulder to see if she was coming out the exit. No luck, so he began circling his car, bending over to inspect nicks that weren't there, squatting by tires he'd checked a couple days ago, and even dropping to his knees and craning his neck to have a look at what he figured was the exhaust system.

Joseph heard footsteps behind him and looked between his ankles to see a pair of jeans and running shoes approaching. He arose quickly and slapped his palms together, as if to knock off the grit and grime that came with car maintenance.

"Everything okay with the car?" Karen asked.

"Oh yeah, I just wanted to have a look and make sure the muffler was okay. I heard a bit of a rattle under there on the way in this morning."

"Want me to have a look? If there's just a loose clamp or a rusty pipe I could probably give you a temporary fix right now—the duct tape special."

Karen rolled up her sleeves as she approached.

"Thanks, Karen, but I think everything's okay, plus I'd hate to see you get dirty."

"Doesn't bother me a bit. With all the time I spend on the beast over there," she motioned toward the immaculate Mustang, "I'm right at home that way."

"It's okay, really. Hey, what are you doing here so late? I thought you marketing types all left early."

"I had to hang around for a while and wait for a call. I'd been nominated for an award for a set of ads I did a few months ago, and I just found out that I won."

"Terrific! Way to go. Who gave you the award?"

Karen waved him off. "Oh just some industry group you've never heard of, but I admit, it sure is nice to be recognized. Being creative in the plumbing supply business is a challenge. I was thinking a celebration was in order, but by the time I got the news hardly anybody was left in the office."

She stopped speaking and smiled pleasantly at Joseph, who

heard a roaring in his ears and felt a thousand years go by before he could form any words.

"It's not much, but could I buy you a drink to celebrate?"

"Why sure, how sweet."

In addition to classic cars, Karen liked good beer. There was a new restaurant and microbrewery by the Falls and they drove there separately. When they'd settled onto a pair of seats at the bar, Joseph followed her lead and order a pint of Flower Power Ale, which he'd never heard of before.

"It used to be that hops were grown in western and central New York, but that ended when Prohibition put an end to legal brewing. This beer is the first to be made with locally grown hops in years, you like it?" she asked.

In truth, Joseph found it too strong and bitter for his tastes, which ran toward a lite beer or two while watching a football game, but he took a good-sized gulp and did his best to keep his face frozen.

"It does have a different kind of taste, a nice change from the usual."

They chatted pleasantly for a while, but Joseph wasn't surprised when it turned out to be too good to last. They were interrupted when Joseph felt a soft hand pressing down on his shoulder. He looked back and his heart sank.

Smith! Did the guy have some kind of tracking system, how'd he know they were there?

With a toss of his head Smith threw the bangs out of his eyes and fixed Joseph with a serious gaze.

"Hi, Karen," he said, without taking his eyes or hand off Joseph. "Can I have just a moment with Joseph?"

"Oh, boy-talk, huh? Sure, I'll go fix my makeup," and she hopped lightly off the stool and headed for the bathroom. Before Joseph could protest Smith tightened his grip.

"Joseph, some heavy stuff is going down at work, you probably heard about it."

Joseph had no clue and, with Karen nearby, didn't much care.

"No, I haven't heard anything, is it something I should know about?"

"Do you think I would make a good sales supervisor?"

"Uh, sure, I suppose, but that's Harsh's job. Did he get a promotion or something?"

"No, not at our company anyway. But he might be encouraged to look elsewhere for the next step on his career path," Smith replied, giving Joseph a meaningful look with nary a blink.

"I don't understand what you mean by that. I thought you and Harsh were friends, aren't you?"

Joseph was confused. After all the time Smith and Harsh spent together, he assumed they were close.

"Things aren't always what they seem," Smith continued cryptically, still not blinking, like a lizard tracking its prey. "Wouldn't you like to work without the call counter, without Harsh yelling at you all the time?"

"Well, I wouldn't miss either one. When is all this happening?"

"It's in the works, Joseph, it's in the works. Just hang tough and don't say a word to anybody, not even Karen. Can I count on you?"

Joseph paused, trying to process what was going on.

"Can I count on you?"

"Sure."

Smith blinked now, and gave Joseph's shoulder a final squeeze.

"Good, and I've got your back, too. I won't be in Harsh's slot long, and you know you're next in line, right?"

"Thanks, that's good to know."

Joseph didn't know what else to say and felt silly about the whole episode. He watched Smith stop briefly to speak with Karen, who was on her way back to the bar, then hurry off.

"What was that all about?" she asked, after settling back onto her stool and taking a pull from her pint glass.

"I think he swore me to secrecy."

"Join the club." She grinned. "I think he's had everybody take the oath at one time or another. Whatever it is, don't take him seriously."

"Sound like good advice."

They went back to chatting and Joseph reflected on how much he enjoyed Karen's company. What was it Gregory had been telling him earlier, that perfume stuff about pheromones? Whatever they are, he thought to himself, bring them on.

Chapter Six

always be the last bug standing

After two pints of Flower Power Ale, Joseph decided the stuff wasn't so bad after all and bought a half-gallon jug of it to bring home with him. On the way he stopped at Tang's for the brown rice and steamed vegetables Monica had requested. She'd insist they eat together, so he ordered enough of the unappealing dish for two, but did sneak in a nice, greasy order of shrimp toast to scarf down on the way home.

Back at the apartment, he turned on the news and poured himself a glass of beer. He hadn't been sitting on the couch long when Gregory appeared on the coffee table in front of him.

"I'm not even going to ask how you got here."

"So, how'd your drink with Karen go?"

"Fine, if you must know. She won an advertising award and we went out for a drink to celebrate, and that's all there is to it."

"I don't know, you sound awfully defensive for an innocent man. Does Monica know?"

"No," Joseph answered, "but I'm sure it wouldn't be a big deal."

Gregory walked over to where some foam had overflowed Joseph's glass and made a small puddle on the table.

"Mmmmm, this is good. Since when did you start drinking decent beer?"

"Hey, I thought alcohol would keep you away."

"No way. One of the favorite roach delicacies is beer. Usually we like it warm and sour, sort of like English beer, but this is okay, too."

"I'm learning way more about roaches than I ever wanted to know. Anyway, Karen recommended the stuff, and it's good."

"Oh, I'm sure. One word from her and you'd be sipping motor oil."

"Look, Gregory, have a heart, she's a great girl."

"Bear in mind that the cockroach heart is nothing more than a pump to move fluid back and forth in our bodies. Why, if my heart stopped working, or was cut right out of my body, I could survive. And that's the difference between us and humans, like I told you with Rule Number Two: We keep our hearts in perspective and aren't run by them. You, though, feel the slightest tremor and think the whole earth just moved for you."

"Alright, alright, I get the drift, enough of the heart stuff. Besides, I've got something more important to ask you about."

"And what's that?"

Joseph described his encounter with Smith at the bar and expressed his surprise at knowing nothing about whatever schemes and plots were going on.

"That's because Smith used to see you as competition; now he thinks he can just make you his underling, like Harshfeld has."

"But does Harsh have any idea what's going on?"

"Probably some. He's not bright, but he's got some primitive survival instincts going. Smith's schemes might not matter to him, though, because Harsh himself is after Lindley's job, and Lindley wants to make vice president."

"If that's all going to happen anyway, then why try to force it?"

"Because none of them want to put in the time or effort to really earn anything. Instead, they'd rather manipulate themselves into higher positions sooner."

"Can they get away with it?"

Gregory made a shrugging motion with his antennae.

"Maybe, but overall manipulation is a bad strategy that usually backfires. Would you like to hear about one of Smith's ongoing efforts at it?"

"Sure, I'm all ears, or should I say my antennae are raised?"

"What Smith does is zero in on people who are unhappy at work. First he sympathizes with them, then he fuels the fire, sometimes even writing up bogus memos with Harsh or Lindley's name on them that criticize the person unjustly and aggravate them even more."

"Why?"

"Once he has them good and stoked up, he just happens to let them know about the confidential complaint process that exists at the head office in Chicago, then walks them through it. Of course, if it comes to anything, he turns the person in on the sly and scores points with the other side, too."

"That's pretty scummy," Joseph exclaimed.

"What's more, I've seen some of the fake e-mail accounts he

sets up and uses to send in complaints about Harsh and Lind-ley. Not just to the head office either, he gets hold of the ad-dresses of company bigwigs, and even the board of directors, and pesters them, too."

"What is it he tells them?"

"Anything he thinks might work. A lot of it is true, too, like paying for nights on the town with company expense money. Harsh and Lindley tell him all about it in secret; he yucks it up with them, then sends the whole mess in, complete with em-bellishments."

"Wow, so why hasn't Smith gotten them fired yet?"

"I'm not sure. He keeps thinking he's on the verge of it, like when he was so cryptic with you, but so far it hasn't worked out for him. Of course, this kind of thing rarely ends well."

"Even if you're good at it?"

"Sure. To really get somewhere you have to focus on what's in your own power to accomplish and stick with it through thick and thin, without getting distracted by things outside your control. That way, you're still in the running when all the plots everybody else launched come crashing down."

"Hmmm, that's a pretty interesting observation."

"Of course. In fact, Rule of the Roach Number Three is based on it: Always Be the Last Bug Standing."

"You mean stay focused and tough it out?"

"Yes, but I don't think you understand the level of commit-ment involved. Just a while ago I mentioned how cockroaches can go right on living without a working heart. Well, it doesn't stop there. Somebody crushes us? Our bodies immediately go into repair mode. A leg gets torn off? We'll grow another. And if our head gets cut off? We'll still keep going—until we starve a month later because we can't eat. Hot, cold, feast, famine, predators, poison, it doesn't matter. Cockroaches keep right on doing our thing, surviving, long after other species wimp out."

"But why so stubborn?"

"What's the alternative?"

Joseph finished off his beer while he pondered this, and then went out to the refrigerator for a refill.

"So how does all that help me with the mess I'm in here and at work?" he asked, while he settled back into the deep cushions.

"Right now you've got a bunch of people trying to run your life in order to help them accomplish some goal of their own. You need to outlast them, no matter how bad it gets. When their schemes are in ruins, you'll be free of the wreckage and still standing."

"My God, Gregory, you make it sound like a disaster movie."

"Good insight, Joseph, a disaster movie is pretty accurate, for what do most people's lives resemble more than that?"

"Bad comedies?"

"Those are a close second, I think."

Suddenly Gregory's antennae rose. "Whoops, I better make myself scarce," he said, and vanished.

"Huh, what's going on?" Joseph listened closely but didn't hear anything, not until a couple minutes later, when the deadbolt turned and Monica came striding in.

"Hey." Joseph waved to her from the couch.

Monica walked over to where he sat and stood over him, glowering.

"What?"

"What are you doing with a jug of beer on your lap and that stupid grin on your face? Have you lost your mind?"

Indeed, there it was. On Joseph's last trip to the refrigerator for a refill he'd decided to just grab the growler itself. Not much was left in it, and all at once he felt the effects of the alcohol, as if Monica was a catalyst.

"A client gave me this and I thought I'd give it a try. You want some?"

"I most certainly do not. It's almost eleven and we both have to be up early in the morning. Where's the food?"

"Right there on the counter. I thought you were coming home at eight, though, so it's been sitting there awhile."

Monica banged around in the kitchen, making a lot more racket than warming up a plate of pasty rice and soggy vegetables called for, Joseph thought. Making sure she wasn't looking, he polished off the rest of the beer.

"I hope you drink more responsibly than this at the picnic Saturday—I don't need to be embarrassed."

"Don't you worry, I'll be the last bug standing."

Monica came into the living room with her plate and sat at the other end of the couch.

"Last bug standing? That makes no sense, you must really be drunk."

"Yeah? Well you can cut out my heart or cut off my legs, but I'll keep on crawling forward anyway."

"You *are* drunk, aren't you, and talking gibberish. I've got something you need to read, drunk or not."

"You know, sweetheart, it wasn't so long ago that you and I would go down the road and tip back a few, remember?"

"That was before I took on real responsibilities and started to build a real career—something you could learn from."

"But we had fun, didn't we?" Joseph asked, leaning in Monica's direction and reaching for her hand.

Monica set her plate down and walked over to the bookshelves on the near wall. She scanned the offerings until she came to one by a popular talk-television psychologist who advocated growing up and leaving the inner child behind.

"Here, this has the chapter you need to look at, maybe it will help straighten you out."

But when she tried to open it to the right chapter, all the pages fell out. Monica just stood in the middle of the room, staring at them.

"I only bought it last year, but there's nothing holding the pages together," she said, sounding confused.

Joseph nodded his head in satisfaction and struggled to is feet.

"One bug's bad advice is another bug's dinner."

a walk in the park

The ball moved through the air so fat and slow Harsh could barely hold himself back until the time was right to take a mighty cut at it.

Whack!

Harsh's second home run of the afternoon arced over the outfielders' heads and came down on the access road, where it took a wicked bounce and disappeared into a thicket of scrubby trees and weeds. Harsh threw back his head and laughed triumphantly. He ran back to the team's bench and grabbed a full cup of beer, then drank it down as he did a leisurely victory lap.

"He'll be bragging about that all next week," Joseph told Karen bleakly.

"He shouldn't," she replied, shaking her head in disgust. "The pitcher we've got couldn't strike out a corpse."

"Probably true, but what can we do? I can't pitch any better, and I doubt any of the other guys can."

Karen looked over their team.

"Probably not, but that doesn't mean all hope is lost."

"What do you mean, are you hoping for divine intervention?"

"No, the men on the team need that, but I used to pitch on my softball team in college, so maybe I can help. You think Ed would be willing to surrender the mound for a few innings?"

Joseph looked over at Ed, who was sweating heavily, badly discouraged, and longing to do nothing more than hang out by the beer kegs.

"I think his ego can handle it; want to fill in?"

Karen trotted out and let a relieved Ed off the hook. She took a few warm-up pitches that were more accurate than his but no faster. The first batter was Smith, who strutted to the plate and hitched up his pants. Harsh and the rest of the guys on their team hooted and howled about a woman being on the mound.

"Hey, honey, it's already four to nothing and it's just the second inning, you looking to invoke the mercy rule?" came a voice from the bench. Smith turned to his teammates and held out his arms, as if to have one so mighty as he hitting against a girl just wasn't fair.

Karen's first pitch came in high, a puff ball ready to be blasted, then took a sudden dive into the catcher's mitt that left Smith reeling when he swung at empty air. He grinned at her like a hungry coyote.

"Okay, Karen, you got away with one good girl pitch, but that's your only gift today. Bring it on."

The next pitch cut through the air like a missile, caught the top of the catcher's mitt, who barely saw it coming, and was over the backstop before Smith knew it had arrived. He stood there, peering through the hair that had fallen in front of his eyes, and examined the empty space around him as if expecting to find the ball suspended there.

Three innings later, after Karen had only given up a single hit, she came up to bat when Smith was pitching. He wound up and launched his fastest underhand right at her head. Karen calmly raised her bat and popped out a bunt that bisected the infield perfectly and gave her an easy base hit. Joseph followed with a double and their team went on to top Harsh's by a score of six to four.

Following the game, when all the players were gathered around the beer kegs, except for Smith, who was off in a corner of the pavilion having an earnest discussion with an unsuspecting young woman who had been with the company for only two weeks, Harsh walked up to Karen and thrust out his hand.

"You struck me out twice and made me fly out the other two times I came up against you; wish some of the guys I got working for me had that kind of game."

She took his hand carefully, as though it might be contagious.

"Thanks, I think, Mr. Harshfeld."

"You want me to go straighten Smith out for trying to bean you like that?"

"It's nice of you to offer, but I could have picked off that pitch in my sleep."

Harsh gave her an appraising look.

"I bet you could have."

Then it was time for him to get back to the beer.

Joseph sidled up to Karen.

"You made it sound like you played some intramural softball, but obviously you did more than that."

"Yup. Division I champs, two years running, but why brag?"

A couple hours later, everybody was spread out with full plates from the picnic buffet when a sixtyish-looking man nobody had taken notice of sat down at the picnic bench where Joseph was eating.

"That's quite a girl you've got, young man, you're very lucky."

"Really?" Joseph said, looking over to the bench under a tree, thirty yards away, where Monica had been whooping it up with her law firm cronies the whole time. She'd scoffed at his suggestion she join his team for softball, pointing at her casual leather shoes that cost more than his monthly share of the rent and were not intended for base running.

"I meant her," the man said, and pointed to where Karen was in the middle of a water balloon fight, picking off everybody in range while she stayed dry.

"Oh, that's Karen, she's great, but I'm living with that one over there," and Joseph pointed to Monica.

"You get along with the suits she's hanging around with?"

"I don't really have much contact with them. I'm sorry, sir, but I don't recall your name."

The man gave Joseph a big, rough hand that came with a walnut-cracking grip.

"Where are my manners? I'm Gary Moses, from Sterling

Builders down on the east coast of Florida. We buy lots of plumbing stuff from you guys and I just happened to be in the area visiting my sister, so, when Lindley invited me, I figured I may as well stop by."

"Sterling? Why, your company went from just a couple houses a few years ago to being one of the biggest builders in the South. At first, Sterling just put in small orders, like for a house or two at a time, but now your company is our largest account. Do you do the purchasing for them?"

"No, nothing that complicated, I own the company."

"You know, I don't have your account now, but I managed it for a while when one of the other salespeople was on maternity leave. I kept up with it after that because I couldn't believe how fast your company was growing. I like how Sterling goes for the good stuff. I mean it's plumbing, people don't look at pipes and things—until something bad happens and they have to—but you don't cut corners. You'd be amazed to know how many of your competitors go for the cheapest junk they can find."

"No I wouldn't," Mr. Moses laughed. "I see the results, and believe me, it ain't pretty."

"Maybe that's part of why you don't need to advertise."

"Now how did you know that?" Moses asked.

"I read a few articles. Sterling is what every builder should try to be. You've made a real name for yourself by being so strict on quality materials and only using your own crews, no subcontractors. Do you and your wife still take care of all the deals and customer contact?"

"Our son, Travis, is old enough to help out now, and he's terrific, but I guess you could say it's still a mom and pop operation."

"You're located in Palm Coast, aren't you, just a few miles south of St. Augustine?"

"We are, and right in the middle of one of the fastest growing counties in the country, too."

"I was in Palm Coast a few years ago. I'd gone to Daytona Beach for a vacation, but I made the mistake of timing it during Biker Week, so I went up the coast and found your town. It's a great area."

"You think so? Well look then, young man, maybe you should think about moving down our way. There's always room for bright young guys there."

"I don't know, I've got the job here, and my girlfriend, and—"

Mr. Moses cut him off. "Take a few days off and have a look around then, and bring your girl with you, and I mean that one over there," he pointed toward Karen, who'd just tossed a water balloon into the pavilion that caught an unsuspecting Lindley between the shoulder blades. "I was a northerner myself way back when, and once I moved down there I never looked back."

"Oh man, I'd love to take a trip to Florida with her," Joseph blurted out.

"Why can't you? Look, here's my card, give me a call if you need a tour guide," Moses said, and handed it to Joseph.

Before they could talk further, a howl arose from the throng milling around the beer keg.

"A cockroach, oh my god, kill it, kill it! It's running, c'mon, stomp the thing before it gets away."

Gregory! Joseph stood up straight.

"Excuse me, sir, but I better tend to this."

"Where I come from we've got roaches the size of birds. You northerners," he said, with a grin and a shake of his head.

Joseph ran over and saw that Gregory was running in crazy, irregular circles on the concrete slab floor the pavilion had been built on. The beer swillers had parted and a bunch of the guys were trying to stomp Gregory, but most were extending their feet like they were testing bath water, not trying to kill anything. Anytime a foot seemed about to land, Gregory changed direction abruptly and headed for safer, at least temporarily, terrain.

Finally, though, it was obvious that Gregory was tiring, and Smith leaped forward, with both feet flailing, to land the fatal blow. Without thinking, Joseph lurched forward and knocked Smith into a buffet table, where his rear end settled into a tray of deviled eggs.

"What the hell are you doing, you freak, you ruined my clothes," he cried out.

"I'm sorry, but I wanted to kill that roach before it got away."

"But I was about to kill that roach; I had him all lined up," Smith bawled, then bawled some more when he pulled the seat of his beige pants around and saw the bright yellow stain.

Harsh stepped forward and addressed Smith. "For God's sake, get it together, it's only a friggin' pair of pants, you baby. Go clean yourself up."

Spotting the smirk that escaped across Joseph's face, Harsh turned on him and continued, "And you ain't so swift yourself. How many idiots does it take to kill a roach?"

A temporary post-battle calm came over the picnickers. Harsh walked back to the plate he'd piled high and picked up a hot dog from the top, still shaking his head and muttering about the idiots he had to supervise. Just as he prepared to take a big bite, he saw a pair of antennae poke free of the relish, followed by a pair of legs struggling to gain a foothold.

"What the hell?"

The bellow of a wounded rhinoceros brought the festivities to a dead stop.

"The roach, the roach! It's on my friggin' hot dog. Oh lord, I'm going to be sick."

He dropped his plate and made a lurching run for the closest Porta-Potty. Smith, seizing the opportunity to redeem himself, charged over and jumped onto the plate, which splattered everything from baked beans to guacamole all over everybody within striking distance. Lindley was so stunned by the glob of chocolate pudding that landed chest-high on his sporty white shirt that all he could do was watch it slide down the front.

With no sign of the bug breaking free, Smith continued to grind the paper plate into the cement with both feet, with a motion that made him look like he was practicing the twist. Once his mission was fully accomplished, he raised his arms in triumph, as though dismissing the vanquished spirits of an entire bug brigade.

A few of the braver souls began inching forward, wanting to

see what, if anything, of the roach was left. They all jumped back as one when Gregory scooted out from under a potato chip and make a break for it. He zigzagged wildly across the cement, like a prisoner breaking free and trying to keep the guards in the towers from drawing a bead on him. At the edge of the slab he bounced off Monica's heel, which caused an outbreak of hysterics that put Harsh to shame, then he disappeared into the grass.

Chapter Eight

even the smallest opening can be a huge opportunity

This early on a Sunday morning the only people out were runners and obsessive dog walkers. The weather forecast called for an unusually warm spring day—later on. Right now, with mist coming off the low, damp ground of the picnic area, a basin shaped like a huge cereal bowl, and the sun barely visible through the trees, there was a chill in the air that made Joseph shiver in his sweatshirt.

He felt like a complete idiot. Here he was, at a time of day when sane people were sleeping or doing nothing more ambitious than drinking coffee and just beginning to pick through fat Sunday newspapers, searching for a talking cockroach. The pavilion used for yesterday's picnic had been stripped down and the garbage carted away. All that remained were the picnic tables and a big sticky spot where the beer had flowed so freely.

After checking closely to make sure no humans were in earshot, Joseph called out, "Gregory, Gregory, you around?" No response. He walked the perimeter of the structure and kept calling. Duck-walking to keep from soaking his pants, he devoted some time to combing through the grass where he thought Gregory had disappeared. Nothing.

"Joseph . . . Joseph . . ." came a faint, weak voice.

"Gregory, is that you, where are you?"

"Up here, I'm stuck."

Joseph scanned the ceiling but saw no sign of Gregory.

"Up where? I can't see you."

"I'm on the beam, up and to your right."

To get a closer look, Joseph dragged a picnic table below it and climbed up. His nose was level with the top of the beam and he scanned it back and forth. Gregory was ten feet away, so Joseph got down and moved the picnic table again. This time he found himself nose-to-nose with Gregory. The roach's antennae drooped listlessly over his head, and his legs were splayed to either side of his body.

"You don't look so good," Joseph observed.

Gregory moaned, "I feel even worse."

In their short acquaintance, Joseph had frequently noticed Gregory, who obviously took pride in his appearance, cleaning himself off. But now he lay in a disgusting miasma of yesterday's picnic spread that almost covered him.

Noticing the look, Gregory explained weakly, "I managed to escape after that idiot, Smith, tried to grind me into the floor, but I was covered in food and my senses barely functioned. I made it into the grass, but then a puppy that seemed to think I was the afternoon entertainment wouldn't stop poking at me with his snout. I got turned around and found myself back by the pavilion, where those bloody murderers were still looking for me. Somehow I managed to get to one of the corner posts, so I climbed up and came out here. It seemed like a safe place. The problem is that I passed out up here and, by the time I woke up, all the gooey stuff had hardened, so here I am," he finished, exhausted from the speech, his voice barely a whisper.

"It's funny, this is how we met, remember, with you stuck and not able to move?" Joseph said, chuckling softly.

"What's so funny about that? I see no humor in being trapped by leftover roofing tar a bunch of humans mistook for food."

"Okay, I'm sorry, but I'm glad you're alright. Do you need me to help you get out?"

"No," Gregory retorted, still miffed, his voice growing stronger, "I can manage."

Joseph watched as Gregory tried to push, pull, and pivot his way out of the mess, but to no avail—he couldn't free a single leg.

"Someone superglue you while you were sleeping?" Joseph asked.

"No, but this marshmallow salad is murder. You could trap a rhinoceros with it."

"Sort of like your own personal roach motel."

"Another joke? Your sense of humor is not a plus here. Maybe I do need some help. You have any ideas?"

"Give me a couple minutes, I'll be right back."

Joseph walked back to his car and retrieved a water bottle from the trunk. He drove to the men's rest room by the main entrance and filled the water bottle with warm water. Back in the pavilion, he gently ran the water over Gregory until the gunk he was ensconced in softened up and fell away. Joseph used the rest of the water to clean Gregory off, with Gregory twisting and turning to make sure the water reached every part of him.

"That feels great, ahhhh, just what the doctor ordered."

Even clean and free, Gregory still moved much more slowly and awkwardly than normal.

"You still don't seem a hundred percent," Joseph observed.

"I'm suffering from a terrible picnic hangover. And look, part of that means I'm feeling awfully dizzy up here, can you help me down?"

Joseph lined up the lip of the water bottle even with the beam so that Gregory could crawl on to it. Carefully he lowered himself and the bug down to the picnic table, where Joseph straddled the attached bench and Gregory made himself comfortable within a small depression in one of the pine table slats.

"You know what I'm curious about," Joseph said, "is why you were running around during a picnic and upsetting everybody, when you've been able to stay hidden at the office."

"A good question, Joseph. That was not my finest hour, not by a long shot. At your office we only come out at night, when nobody's there. We even wait until after the cleaning crew is done. Remember, if you hadn't come in so early that one morning you never would have seen me."

"But this was the middle of the afternoon."

"I was getting to that. Remember the other night, how I told you roaches like warm beer?"

"I think so, but I was enjoying a little too much beer myself at the time."

"Considering who you live with, it can be classified as medication."

Joseph's back stiffened, and then relaxed.

"Think I can get a prescription?" he asked, and laughed at himself.

Gregory cringed at the slight increase in volume.

"Let's agree to use quiet voices, okay? My head feels like it's being blown apart in slow motion. Anyway, I was staying out of sight and napping in the grass, but then I got a whiff of the beer, and what's the harm in having a drink? It was a warm day, the sun was out, and plenty of beer had been spilled—I was swimming in it, literally."

"You and half the company."

"Yeah, but nobody tries to stomp on them. Unfortunately, I drank too much and got dizzy. Next thing I knew I was in the middle of the floor with a bunch of crazed softball players out to kill me."

"They almost succeeded, you know."

"Despite my drunken state at the time, I do know, and I appreciate, how you came forward to stop Smith. He had me in his sights and that could have been the end for me. I thank you most sincerely."

"You're welcome. You know, if anybody had told me the day would come when I'd knock a coworker into a table of food to save a cockroach, I'd never have believed it. But the truth is, roach or not, I like you a lot better than Smith."

"You know what's funny, Joseph? I've heard people in your office call Smith a cockroach before—and I felt insulted."

"Can't say as I blame you. Hey, that was great with Harsh. He turned green and spent about twenty minutes in the Porta-Potty. Tell me you got into his hot dog on purpose."

"Actually, I was just trying to hide. Let me tell you, Joseph, when I saw that mouth of his opening I thought the end had come. My only hope was making sure he saw me, and thank God it worked."

"I've been the victim of that mouth plenty of times myself, and it ain't a pretty sight from any angle, whether words are coming out of it or he's trying to put you in there with lunch."

Joseph and Gregory fell silent for a time. In Gregory's case, he was still struggling to come out of his beer-fog. For Joseph, though, the time was spent reliving the horrors of the previous day. The worst was Monica's fury, especially her screaming at Joseph after Gregory bounced off the heel of her shoe.

"You let that cockroach get away, Joseph, what's wrong with you? You think those things are an endangered species? And look," she pointed at her shoes as though the soiling was perfectly visible, "my new shoes are ruined, ruined! You know what those cost me, don't you? More than you make in two weeks!"

"Monica, there's not a mark on them, how can they be ruined?"

A tall, distinguished-looking man in tennis shorts and a polo shirt strode over and took up a position at Monica's side and patted her shoulder gently.

"Now, now, sweetheart, don't get too upset, we'll have the shoes cleaned and they'll be good as new, I'm sure," he said, fixing Joseph with a withering stare in stark contrast to the soothing voice. "Why, Monica, your toilet salesman is right here, I'm sure he would be happy to replace those shoes. Though, given his line of work, it probably takes a lot to disgust him."

"Hello, Mr. Primson," Joseph lamely addressed Monica's father. "Did you enjoy the picnic?"

"Yes, I did, until this insanity over a cockroach. Were you really trying to protect it?"

"No sir, of course not. I wanted to kill it, too; me and Smith just ran into each other."

"Ran into each other, you say? I hope you two don't form an exterminating business together, the city would be overrun."

Joseph had nothing to say to this, so he shuffled over to the beer kegs and poured himself a cup. It wasn't nearly as good as that Flower Power Ale, he reflected. He scoped out the area in hopes of catching a glimpse of Karen, but she was nowhere to be seen. Smith was off in a corner and holding out the seat of his ruined pants, with the new girl scrubbing at the stain with a wet dish towel and an unhappy grimace on her face.

A subdued Harshfeld came over and joined Joseph by the beer kegs. He poured himself a cup and brought it to his lips. Instead of drinking it, he wrinkled his nose and poured the beer on the lawn.

"Never thought I'd see the day when I did that, no sir," he reflected. Continuing in the same quiet voice, he turned to

Joseph. "Joey, if you'd let Smith kill that roach like he was out to, the thing'd never have gotten in my food, and my food never would've ended up in the can. You get my drift here?"

Harsh looked clammy, and his Guns N' Roses T-shirt, bought in a skinnier era and now stretched tight across his belly, was soaked with sweat.

"I'm real sorry about what happened. It must have been awful."

"Yeah, well, what's really going to make you sorry is work this coming week, because that's going to be awful."

Joseph felt his heart sink at the news. Wasn't work already bad enough?

"You think cold calls are bad? Your share of them is going way up. In fact, I'm going to let Smith and some of the others take over your accounts for now, and you can focus on getting us new business."

"But, Mr. Harshfeld, I'll go broke doing that, without my active accounts," Joseph protested.

"Really? I guess you'll just have to hit the phones running on Monday and drum us up some pretty impressive new business, huh?"

"That's not right and you know it."

"Are you sassing me?"

The aggravation seemed to revive Harsh; his voice strengthened and his cocky posture returned.

"No, I'm not sassing you, but I'm not going to take this sitting down."

"Fine. We'll get you a longer phone cord and you can walk

around while you talk," Harsh said, inching his way toward Joseph until their chests almost touched. "Anything else?"

"What you're doing is wrong. This is no way to be a supervisor."

"Well, well, now the protector of bugs is criticizing me? You either do as you're told or go get another job. You got that?"

Joseph remained silent but held Harsh's gaze.

After Joseph told Gregory all of this, Gregory said, "That's quite a step forward, being able to stand up to Harshfeld like that."

"Some step forward; many more steps like that and I'll be stepping up to the unemployment line."

"And how did things go at home after the picnic?"

"Beautifully, just beautifully. Once Monica got through yelling she stopped talking to me completely, except to say I had to sleep on the couch."

"It looks like you survived the ordeal."

"Yeah. In fact, without her toothgrinding, I slept lots better than usual—except for when Smith called."

"What did he want?"

Joseph told Gregory about the 4 A.M. phone call from a drunk, barely coherent Smith, wherein Joseph was accused of spearheading dark plots against Smith out of jealousy and in order to usurp Smith as the up-and-coming star of the company.

"Don't you mess with me," he'd said, in a menacing slur. "I'll make your life a nightmare, pal, a nightmare."

"Smith, why don't you go sleep it off? I'm not out to get you," Joseph replied.

"Then why'd you throw me in the deviled eggs, huh? You embarrassed me in front of everybody. And don't think I don't know you knew Karen was a ringer."

"What?"

"She's some sort of softball star, for chrise sake, and you used her to make me look stupid."

"Goodnight, Gerald."

"You better watch your back."

"Gregory, in just a few minutes time yesterday, I pissed off my girlfriend, her father, my boss, that nut Smith, and I don't even know who else. I'm sunk," he said, dropping his shoulders and shaking his head regretfully.

"But it wasn't all bad, Joseph. What about that builder you told me about, Gary Moses? He's a big deal."

"He is, you're right, and he's a real nice guy, too, but that's all he was being, nice. What do I have to offer him?"

"Plenty," Gregory replied. "Even though the day seemed like a disaster, the good in it was pretty significant, too, right?"

"Maybe, I don't know."

"What I know is that this brings us to the fourth Rule of the Roach: Even the Smallest Opening Can Be a Huge Opportunity."

"You think?"

"I know. Us cockroaches have made a specialty of making the most of any opening, no matter how small. Do you know that roaches lots bigger than me can fit through openings narrower than the side of a dime?"

"I never thought about it, but I guess that's why you guys are known for getting into everything."

"You got it. Openings that other species walk right by or think are too tough to force themselves through are our meat and potatoes. We go where others won't, and you know what that means?"

"What?"

"We find rewards and opportunities on the other side that are untouched. Take this gentleman, Moses. Sure, it's not a huge door swung open for you to stroll through at your leisure. Lots of people go for those. No, it's an opening maybe just for you; at least, just for you right now. Openings are only opportunities if you act on them without wasting too much time, otherwise the opening closes up, and not even the most determined roach can find a way through."

"That makes sense. Speaking of finding a way, do you need a ride?" Joseph inquired.

"Why, Joseph, this comes as a surprise, aren't you disgusted by me?"

"I used to be, that's for sure, but considering the people I'm dealing with, you don't look so bad in comparison. Besides, how would you get home from here?"

Gregory scrambled out of the table divot and looked around.

"I probably wouldn't, to tell you the truth."

"Hop on board," Joseph said, and turned the water bottle upside down to give Gregory a broader traveling space on the bottom. "I'll drop you off at the office and you can nurse that hangover. Want to stop for a beer on the way? There might be some empties lying around the park with some left in the bottoms."

Gregory groaned. "Right now, I'd rather eat your mother's cucumber salad."

down in a hole

Joseph stared bleakly at the black box whose bright red digital display read a big fat zero. True to his word, not only had Harsh put him on cold calls exclusively, but he'd come in early and hooked up an individual counter to Joseph's phone, along with a longer cord.

"Maybe I can hang myself with the thing," Joseph mused.

He'd been banished to the couch again last night. This morning, after getting up before Joseph and making sure to create enough noise to wake him up and keep him awake, Monica announced she was exercising at the club again this morning, instead of at home, and would go directly to work from there. Joseph was mildly surprised at this, but was relieved to see her go.

At work the few people there when he arrived either ignored him completely or averted their eyes, a practice repeated by everybody who followed. Apparently he was a marked man, and nobody wanted to incur Harsh's wrath through guilt-by-association.

A few useless sighs later, Joseph picked up the phone and began working through the list of names and numbers in front of him, also provided by Harsh. A long morning followed, with hang-up after rude remark after bored message-taking being par for the course. He didn't set a single appointment and only raised the dimmest spark of interest in a handful of people, whom he put on the list of callbacks to follow up with later in the week.

When Harsh stopped by Joseph's desk on his way out to lunch he checked the list and let out a nasty laugh.

"This all you got? I used to do that much in twenty minutes without hardly trying. What's the matter with you, Joey?"

"I dunno, boss, must be the Monday morning flu."

"Being smart again, I see. Well, it'll be a black-and-blue Monday for you when I plant my size thirteen on your butt cheek, you don't start shaping up."

"Yes, Mr. Harshfeld."

Harsh took a long look at Joseph. He'd had plenty of people talk back to him worse, but for Joseph, who he regarded as a wimp anybody could push around, this was way out of character.

The top half of Smith's head appeared behind Harsh's shoulder.

"Joseph, I need some information from you in order to follow through with your accounts. Is it okay if I access your client files? Mr. Harshfeld gave me your password."

Smith's face disappeared, then came back into view to one side of Harsh, where the boss couldn't see him. Smith waved his hands at Joseph and mouthed the words "It's okay."

"Go right ahead, but check back with me if the spelling on the password is wrong," Joseph answered.

Harsh stared hard at Joseph.

"I might have to get in touch with that lawyer girlfriend of yours and have her straighten you out. When she calls, you snap to like a trained monkey."

"What?"

"You think I don't listen in once in a while?" Harsh was grinning now, which made him look like an evil jack-o'-lantern. "She must've neutered you in your sleep."

Joseph remained speechless as Harsh laughed his way out of the huge room, with Smith in his wake and patting one of Harsh's beefy shoulders. At least today, for the first time in months, there hadn't been any calls from Monica for them to listen in on.

Joseph did his best with the phones for a while longer, but his luck didn't improve and he was fed up. If he was doing this bad, what did it matter if Harsh fired him? A sudden inspiration hit Joseph. He would have been too scared to entertain it a week ago, but now he found his feet taking him to the suite of marketing offices, where Karen's was first in line.

"Karen, sorry to bother you, but you got a minute?"

Karen glanced up from her computer screen. She looked annoyed at first, which almost caused Joseph to turn tail and run, but her face broke into a smile when she saw who it was. Looking around her office, Joseph realized he'd never been in here before. The walls were covered with pictures of classic cars, mostly Mustangs and Corvettes, and posters from old horror flicks. Karen's window ledge and bookshelves were adorned with an assortment of wind-up *South Park* characters, who looked out from the edges of books, were hidden in plants, or occupied places of honor on the front of her desk.

"Would you be interested in, I mean, if you're hungry, getting some lunch?" Joseph fumbled, with his breath running out so quickly the last few words barely had the power to leave his lips.

"I thought you'd never ask. Where should we go?"

Not having prepared for success, Joseph's mind went blank, then he stammered, "Alcorn's was good before, how about that?"

"Fine with me. It's too early to drink beer, but just the aroma from the holding tanks is worthwhile. Can you give me a couple minutes to finish up here, and I'll meet you downstairs in the lobby?"

"Downstairs," he repeated, smiling now, and then stumbled back to his desk.

After they found a table and ordered food, Karen leaned forward and squeezed Joseph's forearm, which almost sent him flying from his chair.

"I've got to tell you: Smith going butt first into that tray of deviled eggs was the funniest thing I ever saw. Tell me, were you really trying to get that bug, or just using it as an excuse to put Smith in his place?"

Joseph's blushing skin felt hot enough to catch fire.

"Well, I wouldn't want to hurt him or anything, but . . ."

He shrugged his shoulders and held his hands out, palms up, mostly because he didn't know how to explain his impulse to save a talking cockroach. Karen took this as an admission of guilt.

"I knew it," she said, slapping the table hard enough to rattle the silverware and draw a few curious stares. "Good for you. That should happen to him once a day, at least."

"Wait a minute, I'm confused. I thought you liked him."

"I thought he was okay, but after that cream puff pitch he tried to bean me with, and a few other things, I've turned in my membership card from the Gerald Smith fan club."

"A few other things?"

Karen shared with Joseph how Smith had called her Sunday, starting with an apology and trying to gain sympathy for his tragedy, and then going into his elaborate plotting. Joseph recounted his own call from Smith and all his other picnic-related troubles, culminating with his treatment at work today. Karen mulled the information over as she finished her chicken fingers.

"I think I might have an idea."

"I'll take any help I can get right now. Let's hear it," Joseph answered.

"You know how you said you're not anywhere with the phone calls?"

"Oh man," Joseph groaned, "nobody wants to talk to me; it's like I'm spreading the plague over the phone."

"Well, how about changing your approach to something that gets their attention?"

"And how do I do that?"

"In advertising, our challenge is to try and find ways of com-

municating to people that cut through everything else they're
being bombarded with, something that gets around the filters.
The best thing is to engage them right off, so they want to hear
more."

"How can I do that with plumbing supplies? It's not exactly
everybody's favorite topic of conversation."

Karen picked up her fork and speared the air with it as she
spoke.

"Not usually, which is why if you start with something interesting you've got a good shot."

"Like what?"

"I don't know, some interesting tidbit, a sales promotion. You
know your audience. Go with what you think they might like."

Back in the cubicle and still aglow from his time with Karen,
Joseph decided to give it a try. After all, what harm could there
be in a creative approach? His results couldn't get any worse.
He wrote down a bunch of rough ideas on a sheet of paper and
followed up with search engine queries to gather information.
After developing a few possible scripts, he settled on a simple
one and gave it a try.

The first two people hung up on him before he could get
anywhere, but with the third, after introducing himself, he
seized a pre-hang-up second to say, "Sir, we're running a special promotion today and if you can answer this question,
you'll win."

He heard a heavy sigh on the other end of the line, but the man said, "Okay, I'll bite, go ahead and ask your question."

"Here it is: In what year was toilet paper on a roll invented?"

"What? I thought this was going to be a question on plumbing supplies, like pipes and stuff."

"Why, sir, toilet paper rolls are technically plumbing supplies."

"Okay, I guess so. Let's see, the year toilet paper on a roll was invented. I don't know, but I'll take a wild guess here . . . 1620?"

"Nope. Toilet paper on a roll wasn't invented until 1890."

"Really, now that's a surprise. So late? What did people use before then?"

"Before the company started using glossy photos, Sears catalogues were popular, and, you probably won't believe this, but centuries ago the Vikings used the frayed ends of anchor cables."

"Ouch! That hurts just to hear about it. No wonder they had a reputation for being mean. Just out of curiosity, what would I have won if I got the question right?"

"A conversation with me."

The man let loose a hearty laugh. "But I'm already having a conversation with you."

"See? I knew you were a winner the second you answered the phone."

The approach didn't work with everybody, but it greatly improved Joseph's overall numbers. It greatly improved his mood, too, because he found himself enjoying his job for the first time.

Near the end of the day, Joseph picked up the phone for a final call and saw Mr. Lindley approaching. He put the receiver back in place and waited.

"Joseph," Lindley began, looking and sounding sterner than Joseph had ever seen him, "I wasn't going to say anything, since it is Mr. Harshfeld's job to discipline the sales staff, but after your obnoxious performance at the picnic Saturday I find it disturbing to see you fooling around when you should be working."

"But I am working, Mr. Lindley."

"Young man, you can't be. I just watched you laughing and grinning over here. What's so funny that you find entertainment on the company dime?"

"Nothing, just talking to new customers, Mr. Lindley, new customers."

"I don't believe you. Furthermore, Mr. Harshfeld has discussed with me your worsening attitude of late, and frankly I think . . ."

"Look, here are my callbacks," Joseph interjected, handing Lindley the list of names.

Lindley scanned them once, then read them through again, more carefully this time. His eyebrows crept higher as he perused the information.

"If these are accurate, you are having quite a productive day."

"My best ever, sir."

"In that case," Lindley said, in a much friendlier tone, "I won't tamper with success," and motioned toward the phone. "Laugh away."

Chapter Ten

feast where others see only garbage

The next day, when Joseph arrived for work, he plopped down in front of the computer screen and hit a key so the monitor would light up and he could get on the Internet and check the day's news. This morning something different happened. He hit a key and found a message on the screen:

RULE OF THE ROACH Nº5: FEAST WHERE OTHERS SEE ONLY

GARBAGE.

"What the—"

"Good morning, Joseph," Gregory said, having materialized at the base of Joseph's keyboard. Joseph still wasn't used to Gregory's sudden appearances and yanked his hands back quickly, as if afraid the computer would burn him.

"Sorry about that. We roaches sense other creatures approaching long before they arrive, and sometimes I forget humans are still in their infancy with such talents."

"I know that *I* sure am. Consider me to be in potty training when it comes to approach sensitivity, and one of these days you're going to make me have an accident."

"Oh, please, spare me the drama. Anyway, I see that you noticed the screen."

"I sure did. I'm up to rule five already, huh? Does that make me a prodigy?"

"Compared to most humans, yes, but in roach terms you'd better stick with the potty training analogy, because you're not ready to go without diapers yet."

"Funny," Joseph said, and examined the monitor again. "How did you get this on the screen?"

"I told you before, one of my big friends from downstairs who . . ."

"Jumps on the keys," Joseph finished for him. "I thought you were goofing on me when you mentioned that before."

"Not at all. How else could I type?"

"Look, Gregory, when I stop and think about it, I'm still having trouble with the idea of you talking."

"If it makes you feel better, I do have the roach who jumps on the keys wash first. We are very clean creatures, you know."

"Okay, okay, I just don't want to think about it right now. Besides, I'm intrigued by your newest rule."

"As you should be," Gregory answered. Before continuing, he nestled into a phone cord coil, and then said, "I was happy to see that you acted out a great example of this rule before being taught it; you are indeed making progress."

"Truth be told, it was Karen's idea that I use a new approach on the phone, and she was right, it worked. I never would have thought it up myself."

"She's a very bright girl. I have to admit, there are some humans who seem much more evolved than the rest."

"Okay, how's this for bright: I know what the rule means."

Gregory came out of the coil and stood on top of it.

"Tell me then."

"Harsh gave me a garbage job as punishment. He knew I'd do badly and lose all kinds of income, but he wanted to take that picnic thing out on somebody, and I was an easy target. But Karen showed me how to take a lousy job and turn it into a nice opportunity. Since Monday, I've picked up a bunch of new clients and have all sorts of appointments coming up. My income is actually going to increase, and I bet Harsh won't like that at all."

"No, I'm sure he won't."

"And you know the best part? On Tuesday, I called Mr. Moses down in Florida just to say how much I enjoyed meeting him. We got talking about some of the problems he's having, now that Sterling is so much bigger, with coordinating orders of building supplies so that everything is there on time, but without having to spend a fortune storing them. I gave him some ideas I thought might help him out and left it at that. The Southern section office takes care of his area, so I wasn't trying to steal him as a client, but guess what happened?"

"I don't know, tell me," Gregory answered, his antennae rising.

"You don't? Well, Mr. Moses called the big bosses in Chicago, the guys who actually own the company, and told them either I manage his account or he goes elsewhere. They didn't like it, but what could they do?"

"So here again, we see an example of rule five."

"How so?"

"Everybody ignored Mr. Moses at the picnic. He's a good guy, down-to-earth, and because he doesn't show off his success, nobody had any idea of his significance to your company. You, by being interested and nice to him, found opportunity in what others passed over."

"Yeah, but he's sure not garbage," Joseph protested.

"Not at all, but he *was* passed over as somebody not worth talking to. An important lesson in all of this, I'd say. Don't look now, but Smith is on his way over," Gregory said, and disappeared into a sheaf of papers.

"How does he do that?" Joseph wondered.

Sure enough, Smith stood before him five seconds later, with both hands held up for a pair of high fives.

"Put 'er there, my man, that's some swindle you pulled off."

"Swindle? What are you talking about?"

"What am I talking about, he asks." Smith lifted his head and spoke upward, as though inquiring of a deity there in the false ceiling. "I'm talking about," his full gaze now square on Joseph's face, "how you stole our biggest account right out from under the nose of the Florida guys and there's nothing they can do about it. Not a thing. They're fuming, fuming, my man," Smith finished and held his hands out again.

Joseph rewarded him with one half-hearted high five and said, "I didn't steal anything, Mr. Moses asked for me."

"Sure he did," Smith said, and winked at Joseph.

"I'll tell you the truth: All I did with him is the same thing I'm doing with my cold calling, just treating people in a way they like to be treated."

Smith laughed at what he thought was a joke.

"Ooooh, what management guru taught you that one?"

"Karen."

"Karen, the hot little number with the Mustang in marketing and advertising? The one I struck out with during the game so I won't strike out when it counts, that one?"

"Yeah . . . her."

"That's right, you like her, don't you?" Smith looked at him quizzically. "Even though you're living with that lawyer who's going to inherit daddy's business and make a fortune."

"If she's so great, you can have her," Joseph blurted out.

Smith cocked his head and look at Joseph oddly.

"Why would you say that?"

"You seem so impressed; maybe the two of you are made for each other. What do you think of that?"

"I think I'd better get back to work," Smith said, and hurried off, pausing once to glance back at Joseph before he did a last bang toss and was gone.

"What was that all about?" Joseph asked, certain Gregory was about to reappear, which he did.

"I think you'd better be careful around him."

"Is there a roach rule that covers that?"

"Yes, but first you need the one you just learned to sink in."

"Sure, why overwhelm me?"

"Just be prepared for some changes around here," Gregory said cryptically.

"Like what?"

"I won't say, but see if Harsh is any different within the next few days."

Joseph eyed him suspiciously. "Are you planning something?"

"Just a little community outing, is all."

Chapter Eleven

the trojan hockey bag

It wasn't nearly at the level he deserved to be playing, but Harsh loved his Sunday night men's hockey league games. By himself, he accounted for two-thirds of the team's goals, and his teammates treated him as much like a star as was possible for a beer league.

Smith, who went too far in the butt-kissing department, Harsh thought, had taken on the role of team manager and mascot. He cheered whenever Harsh scored or railed some middle-aged accountant against the boards, groaned whenever one of his shots went wide, and always had pizza, wings, and pitchers of beer ready when the guys came upstairs to the bar after showering.

Fifteen years earlier, Harsh had played a season of college hockey. He never tired of telling people that, though he left out the part about it being a community college. His college hockey career ended in year two, when a combination of bad grades and off-ice assault charges got him booted from the team—and college. And that left the beer leagues.

Tonight's game was huge. A few leagues from the other rinks in western New York, a hotbed for former greats, and his had gotten together and organized a play-down. Teams had to win their leagues first, and then go on to play a series of round-robin games that narrowed it down to the two best. And that is what Harsh was here for tonight. His team and one other had seized the top two spots, and tonight's game was for top beer league bragging rights. He'd been ready a long time.

Ready didn't mean on time. Harsh, especially for important games, liked to show up late, just to get the other guys worried so they'd show a little appreciation when he appeared.

Everybody else was at least half dressed when he strode into the locker room. A chorus of shouts greeted him.

"What happened, a group of NHL scouts try to kidnap you in the parking lot?"

"Oh man, finally, I thought we were going to have to suit up that chubby friend of yours with the weird hair."

"Hey, Harsh, we were worried the other guys had you bumped off so they'd have a chance."

Harsh grinned broadly at his teammates, feeling warmly toward one and all. He dropped his stuff, spread his arms wide, and announced, "I've arrived, you lucky, lucky people."

"Better shift your arrival into high gear, then, because we're running out of time to hit the ice."

Moving quickly and efficiently now, with well-practiced movements, Harsh stripped down in a flash before even opening his hockey bag.

"Boys, take a gander at this," he boomed.

Two days ago, the helmet Harsh had special-ordered six weeks earlier arrived in the pro shop. Not only was it a hard-to-find model from a European manufacturer, but he'd instructed them to decorate it with the team colors, and that took extra time. He could hardly wait to see their reaction when he told the guys he'd done all this because he'd known they'd make it this far. The truth, of course, was that it wouldn't be possible without him. Come to think of it, the team should have thought to get him a special helmet. No matter, it would be a huge hit.

With a dramatic flair, Harsh drew down the zipper and allowed the bag to expand of its own weight. Then, without looking, because he'd packed it on top, he thrust his hand into the bag and grabbed the helmet, fully prepared to draw it out and wield the mighty piece over his head for all to see, a display to shock and awe.

Except something was crawling up his arm.

Cockroaches!

Waves of them!

Frozen, Harsh watched in horror as they scampered up his arm and scattered into the hair that covered his chest and back, then his legs, and places no human should ever have to endure.

The other men stared in disbelief, then ran from the locker room when the bugs came their way.

Two minutes later, the referee came into the locker room, saying, "Harsh, I've heard of psychs before, but your guys are too much. They're out there telling the other team you're covered in cockroaches, what bull—"

The ref's jaws slammed shut when he saw it was true. He stood there staring, his legs trembling and unable to move, until a lone cockroach ambled to within a foot of his skate; then he made a desperate sprint for it, skates and all.

Twenty minutes later, Harsh remained in the shower, convinced he still hadn't rinsed them all away and feeling tiny legs everywhere, making pilgrimages over his entire body, when Smith came in, moving gingerly and ready to bolt at the first sight of anything that wasn't human.

"Hey, Harsh, your team had to forfeit, the game's over."

Smith was sure Harsh had heard him, but there was no response. He moved to the head of the shower room but couldn't see in; the steam rose thick from the hot water coursing through the showerheads full blast.

"Harsh, you in there, you okay?"

"It was him," came a grim voice surprisingly close by. Startled, Smith stepped back a few paces.

"Him who?"

"The roach from the other day, that's who."

"What are you talking about?"

"The lead roach coming up my arm, it was the same one from my hot dog, at the picnic."

"C'mon, I know you've had a scare, but you've got to keep it together."

"It was him, I tell you, I'd know him anywhere. Man-oh-man," he groaned in agony, "what a nightmare. Are the rest of the guys still here?" Harsh asked hopefully.

"Nope. They all went home."

"What about you, Smith, you want to stick around for a beer or six?"

"No can do, Harsh, I need to get going."

Harsh nodded to himself in the shower.

"It was the same friggin' bug," he muttered darkly. "I'd know him anywhere."

grow eyes in your back

"Have you heard?" Joseph asked Gregory.

It was 7 A.M. Monday morning. Soon into his new phone strategy of the previous week, Joseph had learned that most of the business owners and higher-ups he needed to talk to started work early, and it was easier to reach them before the receptionists came in and started weeding out calls like his.

"Heard what?" Gregory responded.

"Late last night, I got a call from Mr. Lindley. He's forgiven me now that my numbers are so good, by the way. From what he said, Harsh had some kind of meltdown and won't be in for a few days."

"Did he give you any details?"

"Not really, just mentioned that the stress was getting to Harsh and that he might have some emotional problems the company didn't know about. Big surprise, anybody who spends time with him can see that Harsh's emotions are about as stable as sweaty dynamite."

"Under the circumstances, I can see why Mr. Harshfeld reacted as he did," Gregory reflected.

Joseph narrowed his eyes and looked closely at Gregory, who

was lounging next to the pencil sharpener in a nest of stray shavings.

"Did you have anything to do with whatever happened?"

"It's not my fault he can't take a joke."

"A joke? It turned a human pit bull into a basket case. C'mon, tell me what happened."

"Only if you promise not to get angry. I know I shouldn't have interefered like that, but you've got to remember, the guy almost ate me."

"That was an accident and you know it."

"Doesn't make the experience any less traumatic," Gregory sniffed, "but alright, I'll tell you about it."

And with that Gregory hopped to his favorite perch atop the pencil sharpener and told the whole story.

Late Friday afternoon, Gregory had snuck into Harsh's brief-case and hitched a ride home. He wasn't surprised to find that the briefcase Harsh carried to and from work every day was al-most empty, except for some off-track betting slips and a copy of the *Sports Illustrated* swimsuit edition. From that evening until game time Sunday, Gregory got to know the large roach clan that inhabited Harsh's house. It turned out that a number of them were distant relatives, so he had a good in.

At first, they were reluctant to go along with Gregory's plan. Harsh provided them with a perfect environment. A complete slob, he left food and dirty dishes all over the place. Because he lived alone in a large ramshackle house he'd bought as an investment after seeing a late-night infomercial that promised easy wealth through real estate—then couldn't sell at anything close to a profit—the roaches had the run of most of it. He kept mostly to the bedroom and living room, where the entertainment system was. But after Gregory promised the services of his clan in return—and he had extensive connections in the roach world—they decided to go along.

As game time approached on Sunday, four hundred roaches filed into Harsh's hockey bag. It was a brave undertaking, for the smell of the bag was so foul that many of the troops complained of chemical warfare. As their general, Gregory instructed them to stay put until he gave the signal to swarm.

When the time came, Gregory led the charge, running straight up Harsh's arm and looking him in the eye. The plan unfolded with precision. The roaches fanned out all over Harsh's body and into every nook and cranny. Then, on the next command from Gregory, they retreated into the cracks where the floor met the wall. This way, everybody apart from Harsh, his teammates, and one referee would doubt their tale of a roach attack. After all, where were they now? And how come there wasn't a single body? Harsh had given the bag a furious cleaning, but while he showered afterward the troops from his house snuck into a side compartment on his hockey bag and returned home with him. Gregory burrowed into Harsh's shirt collar.

Returning home was easy for Gregory. The roach invasion had sent Harsh into a paranoid frenzy, and he convinced himself the incident was the opening salvo of an attack that had something to do with work, since he'd first seen the roach at the company picnic. He went directly from the rink to his office and took everything he could think of that could be used against him, or that possessed leverage he could use to cling to his job.

Just for good measure, Gregory, as Harsh brooded in his chair, ran out from under his collar and onto the tip of Harsh's nose. There, he reared up on his hind legs and fluttered his wings and wiggled his antennae. In a cross-eyed fit of horror and fury, Harsh threw a devastating punch at the roach. Gregory, who felt it coming before Harsh even finished winding up, jumped off his nose and escaped into the motor casing of the nearby mini refrigerator.

Gregory paused to watch Harsh smack himself in the nose and flop backward into his chair, where the momentum caused it to topple over and send him sprawling to the floor. For the next hour, Harsh just lay there, groaning and holding his broken nose with both hands.

"I don't know if that was the right thing to do or not, but I can't say as I feel sorry for him," Joseph observed. "He's made life miserable for plenty of people here, not just me."

"He has indeed," said Gregory. "We roaches of this building rank him as among the worst of the humans here."

"Among the worst? Who could be worse than him?"

"Smith, for starters."

"No, not Smith, he's just pathetic, not dangerous."

"Joseph, with Harsh, at least he comes right at you. Smith is the kind who will forever try to launch conspiracies and plots behind everybody's backs, with no real allegiance to anybody but himself."

Joseph reflected on this a bit.

"True, but everybody knows he's a creep. That's probably why none of those company complaints he's been making have gone anywhere."

"That doesn't make him any less dangerous. In fact, my concern over events here leads me to accelerate your education. Are you ready for another Rule of the Roach?"

"Lay it on me," Joseph said, and leaned back in his chair with both hands clasped behind his head.

"Here it is: Grow Eyes in Your Back."

"I've only seen that happen in horror movies—you know, with genetic mutations running wild?"

"Very funny, but I'm sure you know better than to take it literally. So tell me, what do you think the rule means?" Gregory asked, addressing Joseph as a professor would a student who has finally shown sparks of intellectual prowess.

"Since you were just warning me about Smith, the rule must mean to be aware of what people are doing behind your back, like scheming to do something that'll harm you."

"Not bad, you've got part of it. See, we roaches have a kind of early warning system."

"You mean your antennae?"

"No, those are good close in for picking up what's going on, but only for a few inches. Here, take a look at this," Gregory said, and turned to display his backside.

"Whoa, now hang on a second, no way am I checking out a cockroach's butt."

"Oh, and you think yours is something special? What I'm trying to show you are the pair of feelers there; each one is covered with small hairs that feed information to the individual nerves that run to each feeler."

Joseph had turned his head away, but now looked from the corner of his eye and spotted what Gregory was talking about.

"Okay, I see them, can you turn back around now?"

Gregory complied, then said, "They function like motion detectors and pick up everything from other creatures' movements to air currents. I know something is coming long before it gets to me."

"But what about the day we first met, when you were on the wrapper when I picked it up? I'd opened the desk drawer and put my hand in and you didn't notice anything until it was too late, and I wasn't even trying to sneak up on you."

Gregory made a pair of quick circles on top of the pencil sharpener and came to stop, saying, "This is embarrassing to admit, but a good lesson for you. Even with all this great equipment, I'd become complacent and failed to pay attention. I assumed nobody would ever be in so early and I didn't bother paying attention to anything more than feeding my face. It could have been a fatal mistake—just like the fatal mistake you'll make if you think Smith is just a creep who poses no real threat."

"But I don't have a rear end with a motion detector growing out of it."

"There you go being silly again. You know what I mean—pay attention to changes in your environment: people doing things differently, treating you differently, shifts in the pecking order, and anything else you can pick up on. You've got the equipment, Joseph, you've just got to fire it up."

"And what do I do with the information I pick up on? I'm not a devious guy, as you've probably noticed. How can I compete with people doing things behind my back? I don't do stuff like that."

"You don't have to act the same way. Just don't sit still and let somebody sneak up and squash you. With roaches, when we detect something coming, the first instinct is to get out of the way. We react faster than humans can blink their eyes. Once you're safe, at least temporarily, then you can plan your own move. Remember, though, survival comes first."

"I guess I've gotten too used to being a sitting duck, or at least a trained one."

"That's a good way to end up being somebody else's dinner. As my grandfather used to say, dodge the exterminator and live to fight another day."

over easy

While Joseph and Gregory talked, Gerald Smith and Monica Primson were having their own meeting, over breakfast, as they had been doing every morning for a week straight now. The restaurant was an upscale place called Dickenson's and was located in the lobby of the building Monica worked in, and that her father, as managing partner of Primson and Chase, owned.

Monica took a bite of her egg white, fat-free cheese, and spinach omelet while she watched Smith dig into a stack of low-carb pancakes that soaked up every bit of the sugarless syrup he'd drenched them in at an alarming rate.

"How much longer should I let Joseph sponge off me before I kick him out? He's becoming intolerable."

Smith interrupted his eating to place a comforting hand on her wrist, saying, "I know it's hard, but let's get things squared away at the company first, then we can do a number on Joseph."

Monica sighed and shook her head.

"I really thought he had potential. I mean, I knew he was kind of wimpy and unfocused when we met, but I thought I saw some real character and intelligence there just waiting to come out. But I guess I was wrong. In the last two weeks, his true colors have been coming out, and I don't like them one bit."

Smith nodded his head sympathetically.

"He's been the same way at work, Monica, and remember what he did to me at the picnic—it was an attack, is what it was."

"Is your back still bothering you?"

"My back?"

"The day after, when we first talked, you said your back hurt."

"I think it's okay, why?"

"Well, I talked it over with Dad, and we think, in light of your injury, that the company could avoid a lawsuit by better compensating you."

His breakfast no longer important, Smith shoved the plate to one side and put his elbows on the table and rested his chin on balled-up fists.

"I do have a high threshold of pain and normally just work through any kind of injury, but now that I think about it, this back of mine is causing some nagging pain. Should I see a doctor?"

"We can certainly recommend one."

"The thing is, like I told you last night, I've already got Harsh's job sewn up."

"You sure about that?"

"Yup. I called Lindley right after the game and told him all about how Harsh was screaming about cockroaches attacking him, but I didn't see a single one in there, and neither did the rink manager."

"But you said his teammates backed up his story about an army of roaches coming out of his hockey bag."

Smith waved it off.

"Of course, but they're his buddies, what do you expect? I told Lindley the experience with that cockroach at the picnic must have made him snap. He must have been under more stress, or had lots more problems, than anybody knew. I had that rink manager call Lindley, too, just to back up my story."

"So you said, but how long can you keep Harsh out? He seems like a pretty determined kind of guy."

"Lindley has me in his place starting today. Believe me, Harsh won't be back."

"Why aim so low, then?"

"Excuse me?"

"Like I told you, we can have you compensated at work in return for your not suing over your injury. But it's not Joseph you should be blaming; he's small potatoes. Lindley is the district manager and in charge of the office, so the buck stops there."

"And maybe somebody new needs to make change for it?"

Monica laughed softly at the joke.

"I think in every race the time comes to hand off the baton to the runner whose turn it is."

Now Smith reached for her and they held hands under the table, discreetly.

"You're something special, you know it?" he said, and gave her knee a squeeze.

She moved his hand away and replied, "It's nice to finally be appreciated."

Like a superstar who had been waiting impatiently offstage for his introduction to be completed, Smith swept into the sales area seconds after Mr. Lindley announced he was taking over the supervisor position while Harsh took some time off to attend to "personal matters."

Lindley looked befuddled when right after he finished addressing the salespeople grouped in front of him with the line, "This is only temporary and we all wish Mr. Harshfeld a speedy recovery," Smith was at his elbow, moving him off without actually pushing him.

"Thank you, Mr. Lindley, and may I say that I appreciate the opportunity to fill in for Mr. Harshfeld. We all hope the big guy gets better soon and rejoins us, right?"

A chorus of muttered "sures" and "whatevers" came from his small audience.

"Okay then, let's get to work."

In his new capacity, a puffed-up Smith was at Joseph's cubicle within minutes.

"Joey, we're taking you off the phones. In the notes Harsh left last week outlining shifts in responsibility, he had you down for auditing all the new and existing sales accounts."

"You can't be serious, Smith."

Smith inched closer to where Joseph sat and lowered his head to be at eye level with him.

"I'm serious as a heart attack, Joey, and Harsh also noted his concerns about your attitude lately. I'm doing you a favor here by telling you that you're on real thin ice."

Joseph could smell the gel in Smith's hair, which now hung just inches from his face, and it was vile, like he'd soaked his head in a vat of industrial toxins.

"Smith, Harsh never wrote notes on anything in his whole life; the guy can barely spell his own name. This is baloney and you know it. An account audit will take weeks; so will my salary increase to make up for lost commissions?"

"To begin with, you are not to insult Mr. Harshfeld behind his back. Secondly, you are not getting an increase in pay, so you'll just have to work fast so you can start generating commissions again. Thirdly, if you refuse, I will see to it that you are fired—today. You got that, Joey?"

Smith jerked his head up abruptly, which caused a piece of hair gunk to land on Joseph's wrist. Joseph yanked his hand back like it had been burned.

"You're insane, Smith. Even Harsh wasn't this bad. And what's in your hair, Agent Orange?" Joseph asked, wiping the foul stuff off with his sleeve. Smith ignored the question.

"Are you refusing your assignment?"

"I'll think about it."

"By the end of the week I want a report on your progress so far. If it's not on my desk, we will fire you. Do you understand me?"

"Oh, I understand you, and better than you think."

"You don't even have a clue," Smith replied, with a nasty chuckle.

Joseph didn't think his day could get any worse, but it did.

When he stepped into Karen's office later in the morning, they started off with a pleasant chat that was lifting his spirits, but they were soon dashed.

"Joseph, I have something to tell you."

"What, that you're going to elope with Smith?"

"Yes, how did you know?" she said, and flashed him a quick smile. "What it is, is that I've been looking for a new job and am pretty sure I'll have some good offers this week."

Along with being stunned, Joseph felt stupid; he'd had no idea she was even thinking about leaving.

"But why leave? You're doing great here; you're the star of this whole department."

"That's sweet of you to say, Joseph, but this whole department is part of a plumbing supply company. It's time for me to do something a little more challenging."

She had a point, and Joseph knew it couldn't be argued, so he told her, "Whoever gets you is going to be one very lucky guy . . . er, I meant to say, company."

"Did you?"

"Did I what?" a badly flustered Joseph answered.

"Mean to correct what you said about a guy being lucky to have me?"

"Oh, that, well, gee, just look at you, you're perfect," he sputtered.

"Why thanks, you're pretty special yourself," Karen said, looking him right in the eye, then voicing concern. "Joseph, your face is beet red, are you okay?"

He nodded his head, saying hoarsely, "Yeah, I'm fine, I just got a piece of bagel stuck in my throat, so I'm going to get some water."

Then he fled.

move while your enemies mull

"That was pretty smooth."

"Look, Gregory, I don't want to hear about pheromones. Karen is special and she's going to leave before I have a chance."

"A chance at what?"

"To be together, of course. But first I need to tie things up with Monica, who I think hates me now, and then I've got to get stuff settled here on the job, and then . . ."

"And then you'll lose her because you farted around too long."

Gregory had followed Joseph into Karen's office, justifying it afterward by saying, "If there can be flies on the wall listening in, why not a cockroach?" and wasted no time critiquing the performance back in the cubicle, after the rest of Joseph's fellow employees went to lunch, leaving a despondent Joseph to stare at the floor.

"But Gregory, you don't understand, all of this takes planning, and a lot of thought."

"No, leave all the complicated planning to people like Smith. You need to come up with a simple strategy and act on it, immediately."

"Uh oh, I feel another Rule of the Roach coming on."

"Right you are, and it's an important one: Move While Your Enemies Mull. For our size, cockroaches are the fastest land animals going—we can move more body lengths per minute than any other creature. Not only that, but we can change direction many times in a single second. So when our enemies are still figuring out where to go, or even after they have started, we move faster and negotiate obstacles better."

"You know, Gregory, I hate to admit it, but that's sort of like what Smith did with getting Harsh's job. He acted fast and succeeded."

"In part, I suppose, but Smith mulled a long time before he moved. Somebody using a roach-like approach would have easily outrun him a long time ago, and you can still one-up him in a big way now."

"How? He's already dug in."

"Maybe, but he's also vulnerable because he thinks he's winning a great victory and is all involved in mapping things out. It hasn't occurred to him that there is still an opening for a competitor to jump in and beat him to the punch."

"By that you mean me."

"Exactly, and the same goes for Karen, though she's not your enemy, of course."

"How's that?"

"She's looking around for a new job, right?"

"Yeah, you heard her."

"So why not provide her with a better opportunity?"

"Nice thought, but how do I do that?"

"That's for you to figure out."

"But Gregory, doesn't working things out with Karen conflict with that other rule, about not listening to your heart?"

"Not at all. Now you know her and have good reasons. Before it was just blind biology, and that gets humans in lots of trouble."

"I don't know. It seems like I have to come up with some kind of masterstroke here, and do it fast, even though I have no idea what it is."

"Unfortunately, humans can't use their feet to help them think, like roaches do, but you can think *on* your feet—so get moving."

Completely flummoxed and unable to think of anything, Joseph forced himself to begin the account audit. Usually it was done when salespeople reviewed each other's work, then the CPAs came in and checked everything over. The idea was to make sure the order amounts were right, the commissions calculated correctly, travel expenses reasonable, the customers made happy, and, in general, that there was a clear and honest paper trail.

Feeling spiteful, Joseph started with Smith's accounts, and it didn't take long to discover they were riddled with inaccuracies. They looked okay on the surface, which is probably how they got past the accountants, but to Joseph's practiced eye a lot of bad stuff was obvious. Not only did Smith inflate sales when calculating commissions, he also fudged travel expenses and submitted bills for dates a quick check showed he hadn't been out doing company business on. Best of all, Joseph saw that Smith was not the leading salesperson. Joseph had beaten him every single month—once the numbers were made honest.

Further inspection revealed Harsh and Lindley signing off on a lot of questionable items. Not just for Smith, but for their own activities. Joseph was supposed to be sticking to salespeople, but since Smith had given him access to all the financial records, why not check them out? He kept at it a couple more days and soon had enough material to cause some major explosions.

After a lot of thought, Joseph came up with a plan, which he revealed to Gregory.

"My goodness, Joseph, you've been doing your homework, haven't you?"

"I sure have, but what I found and what I'm going to do about it are frightening. I have to admit I'm scared."

"Nothing wrong with that. The important thing is that you are making moves, moves that nobody else anticipated."

"What I can't figure out is why Smith had me go through these records when there was so much there to nail him on."

"Any thoughts on why?"

"I don't know. Maybe he thought I'd just quit, or maybe he thinks he's so much smarter than me that I'd never figure out what he did—or be too scared to do anything about it."

"And you are doing something about it?"

"It looks that way. I contacted corporate headquarters in Chicago and, though it took some explaining, I finally got put through to the right guy and gave him enough information so that he wants to meet with me in person. I fly out tomorrow. Smith thinks I'm going on a sales appointment I set up a long time ago and couldn't get out of."

"Good thinking."

"Thanks. Oh, and another thing, I went back through the Sterling Builder records again, only with a fine-toothed comb, and you know what I found?"

"Dandruff?"

"Even worse. The bigger builders get all kinds of discounts and special treatment, since they order so much at once, but the rep in the Southern office never bothered to adjust commission and discount rates for Gary Moses when his business grew, so he's been paying a lot more than he needs to for a couple years now."

"Is that part of the Chicago trip, too?" Gregory asked.

"No. Actually, I got in touch with the finance guys, who put the company CPAs right on it. Getting nailed for fraud would sink the company, so Moses is going to get his money back, and then some."

"So you struck a blow for the good guys. Keep it up."

"Let's just hope I can keep it up in Chicago."

"I wish you the best with it; you'll do great."

"I can't believe I'm asking this, but do you want to come along with me, for moral support?"

"Sure, and I'll get to make my first airplane flight, too."

"Will that make you the first airborne roach?"

"Oh no, plenty of my relatives fly all the time. Real jet-setters, you might say. There are even a few roaches who made it into outer space."

"What, now roaches are going to spread out through the universe?"

"Who knows, maybe Earth was just a starting point. One small step for man, one great leap for all roach-kind."

the firm

On the flight to Chicago, Joseph envisioned a big-deal meeting, with a large number of grave-looking and obviously prosperous men listening to him intently, then grilling him the same way. At the head of a vast and hugely expensive table, Joseph would calmly lay out the numbers to his stunned audience.

It didn't work out that way.

Instead, Joseph was ushered into a plain office inhabited by the vice president for corporate oversight, Daniel Spector.

"Hello, Joseph, won't you have a seat?" Mr. Spector motioned to the two in front of his desk.

"Thank you, Mr. Spector, and I appreciate you making the time to see me so quickly."

"Please, just call me Dan. Let's cut to the chase. You made some extraordinary claims over the phone. Can you back them up?"

Joseph unzipped the carrying case on his lap, removed the fifty-page report he'd painstakingly prepared, and placed it, along with a CD copy of the same report, on Dan's desk. The man looked harried, as if this was intruding on an already overloaded schedule, but he nodded and took the report in his hands and immediately began scanning it. As he flipped back and forth through the contents, Dan made a series of grunts and tongue clicks, but Joseph couldn't tell from his flat poker face what they meant. Ten silent minutes passed before Dan dropped the report on his desk and leaned forward to scrutinize Joseph more closely.

"You have done a remarkable job here, son. Everything is well documented and very clear. Normally, because your company is such a small part of what we do, I'd kick it back to the local district manager, that Lindley fellow, and instruct him to straighten it out. But it appears as if he's part of the problem, yes?"

"It looks that way, sir, I mean Dan, at least from what I could tell."

"Well, small potatoes or not, this kind of stuff makes the whole organization look bad, so I'll be out there with a team of my best guys on, oh . . ." He looked over his calendar, ". . . next Monday morning. How's that?"

"I think that's terrific. You must have a lot of questions I can help you with."

To Joseph's surprise, Dan said, "No, actually I don't. I've got to get out there and get the lay of the land myself," and with that, he got up, gave Joseph's hand a hearty shake, and escorted him back out to the waiting area. With a final clap on Joseph's shoulder, he said, "See you Monday, and good work, we appreciate it."

Before Joseph could thank him, Dan was gone. Their whole encounter had taken twenty minutes. Feeling disoriented by the brevity of it all, Joseph just stood there and looked around, as though in a foreign country.

"Do you need directions to the elevator, sir?" the receptionist asked him.

With their cab driver blasting some kind of godawful music that sounded like John Tesh on speed on the other side of the thick partition, Joseph began reviewing the meeting with Gregory, who had heard the whole thing from an inside pocket of Joseph's carrying case.

"Look, Joseph, that the meeting was short isn't a bad thing; you got his attention and he's coming right out, in person, so you must have impressed him with what you had."

"You think?"

"Yes I do. You accomplished exactly what you came here for. The shortness of your time there is probably a good indication of how strong your case is."

"I hadn't thought of that," Joseph said, his spirits lifting as he relaxed from the tension of the meeting and considered what it meant. "I guess I got it right, huh?"

"You certainly did, and congratulations, you made a strong move instead of waiting and allowing yourself to be at the mercy of events over which you'd given up control. How does that feel?"

"A lot better than being a dodo bird."

The rest of their trip was uneventful. Joseph snuck Gregory out to watch a movie with him during the flight and they landed back in Buffalo at 6 P.M., right on time. After dropping Gregory off at the office, Joseph headed home. He wondered to himself, should he tell Monica? He'd promised Mr. Spector to keep it to himself, but she'd be impressed to see that Joseph had finally stood up for himself and done the right thing.

Or so he thought.

Upon entering their apartment, Joseph was greeted by the sight of a pile of his stuff in the middle of the living room floor.

"Monica," he called out, "what's going on here?"

She swept into the living room with an armful of his clothes and dropped them onto the pile.

"It's time for you to move on, Joseph. I've arranged your things here for you and will allow you two days to remove them before I change the locks. And don't take anything that isn't yours. I have a complete list of my belongings and will make your life a nightmare if you take anything of mine or damage my apartment in any way."

Joseph looked at the jumble of stuff she claimed to have arranged and said, "Living with you *is* a nightmare. Two days is fine."

She pulled up short.

"What? I can't believe you just said that. You've got some nerve, after all I . . ."

Joseph didn't hear the rest of it because he'd suddenly become aware of a scent that, while familiar, had never been a part of this dwelling. What was it? That scorched, sickly odor . . . ?

Smith!

Now he was starting to get it. Joseph grinned broadly and

felt a surge of relief. Ignoring whatever she was babbling about, he asked, "So when was Smith here?"

"Smith, the gentleman from your work? Why would he be here?"

"C'mon, Monica, I smell him. What's going on, you two hook up?"

"Typical, Joseph, just typical of you to be gross and trivialize things. Yes, if you must know, he has been here. I felt sorry for him after you injured his back at the picnic and we've become quite fond of each other. He's really an extraordinary man."

"Oh he's extraordinary all right. Look, you two deserve each other and I won't interfere. I'll take a load of my stuff now and come back for the rest tomorrow, okay?"

"Okay, but there is something else you need to know. I am now chief counsel for your company, soon to be your former company, I might add," she threw in cryptically, "so I advise you not to retaliate against Mr. Smith."

"Chief counsel is it? I thought you specialized in ambulance chasing."

"Do not denigrate my practice, Joseph. Daddy approves of Gerald and me and has assigned me the account. It will broaden my experience."

"You've got that right, your new account is going to bring you some surprising experiences all right."

Monica put her hands on her hips and looked Joseph up and down.

"And just what is that supposed to mean?"

Joseph smiled and left her with the parting words, "I'll let you find out, and I hope Smith can tolerate the toothgrinding."

She opened her mouth to let him have it, but Joseph was already out the door.

rest up to wreak havoc

In his haste to leave, Joseph forgot about taking any of his things, but he didn't want to go back now. Oh well, he hadn't worn these clothes to work, so they'd do him for another day. He needed to find a hotel and, reasoning that they were cheaper near his office, decided to head out that way and stop off to speak with Gregory first.

After making sure nobody was there working late, Joseph walked to his cubicle and began calling, "Gregory, Gregory, are you here?" After repeating himself a few more times, Gregory appeared from the base of one of the dividers and ambled over to Joseph's feet.

"What is it?"

"You sound sleepy, did I wake you?"

"Yes, in fact you did, now what's so important that you have to disturb the beauty sleep of a poor old roach?"

"That reminds me, I was wondering a while back how old you are."

"A few days ago I celebrated my five-month birthday."

"That's all, five months? Why, you're just a baby."

"Wrong, Joseph," Gregory said wearily. "A five-month-old

human is a baby, but my life span tops out at six months, so I'm getting up there."

"Man, six months? That's no time at all."

"It does feel that way, I admit."

"But wait, that means you're only going to live another month."

"I may last a little longer; I do take good care of myself, you know."

"But I need you; I'm just starting to get it together, finally, after all these years. You can't just move on like that."

"You'll be fine, Joseph. We're nearing the end of your lessons and you're doing a lot better than you think."

"Really? I feel as mixed up as ever."

"It will all turn out well for you, Joseph, I have faith in you. And to demonstrate that, how about another Rule of the Roach?"

"If you think I'm ready."

"Given that you've come in here ready to overthrow your bosses at the soonest possible second, I think the next lesson is important for you to have now."

"Let's hear it then."

"Here it is: Rest Up to Wreak Havoc."

Joseph sat in his chair and reached back to massage his neck while he thought over the new rule.

"Weren't you telling me not long ago to be aware of what was going on and react to it quickly? I don't remember rest being part of the equation."

Making his way toward the desk, Gregory climbed up the wastepaper basket and perched on the lip of it to make himself more easily heard.

"That's right, and it's exactly what you have done so well. But, in addition to being alert to what's going on and reacting fast when you need to, it's also important not to fly off in so many directions at once that you exhaust and distract yourself to the point of failure."

"So what do you suggest?"

"Ask Karen out on a date for this weekend."

"What, with everything that's going on?" Joseph replied, and he filled Gregory in on how Monica had given him the boot.

"Joseph, that's my point, nothing is going on this weekend. You took care of what you needed to; the next step won't happen until Monday, so relax. Find a place to hole up for now, and have some fun."

"You know, I never thought of asking her out."

"You couldn't have, but now that Monica has thrown you out, you're free. Get your stuff and get settled in somewhere. Get together with Karen and have fun. Get plenty of rest. And get your mind off of work."

"You're starting to make sense."

"I've been making sense since the instant we met. Do you know how much roaches sleep?"

"I never thought about it. I don't know, a few hours a day?"

"Nope. About eighteen hours a day. Usually we just take

care of what we need to at night, then sleep the rest of the time."

"But I've seen you around at all times of day."

"True, but that's only because you've become a special project of mine. Once we're done, I'm catching up on my sleep. Remember this, it is the ones who are constantly running around without resting up or taking breaks who are the most vulnerable, for most of the motion is simply energy wasted trying to keep up with their own disorganized thinking. If you come in ready, rested, and with a solid plan, but prepared to switch up as needed, you'll prevail."

"But there's so much I could do over the weekend."

"No there's not. Think of yourself right now as a designated hitter. You don't need to be out running laps while the game is going on. Just be prepared to step up and swing with all you've got when the right pitch comes."

After allowing Gregory to amble off to dreamland, Joseph left the office and wheeled back out onto Niagara Falls Boulevard to find a hotel. The tourist season was a few weeks off so plenty of rooms were available; the challenge was finding a good one. Since he might be staying put for a while before settling on a new apartment, Joseph focused on the cheaper offerings, which were mostly single-floor wood buildings with a handful of rooms that might have been charming in the 70s, but were now just hanging on in hopes of attracting tourists who wouldn't be back soon enough to make service a worry.

He settled on one that looked clean and checked in. Not too bad, he thought, as he surveyed the room. Nothing fancy, but it would do just fine. Having splurged on another growler of Flower Power Ale on his way to visit Gregory, he walked across the parking lot to the small lobby in search of an ice machine.

The proprietor sat behind the desk with his large belly pushed right up against the computer keyboard. Joseph heard screams and roaring engines coming from the tiny speakers.

"Redneck Rampage," the man said, as though Joseph had asked what game he was playing.

"Excuse me?"

"That's the name of the game I'm playing, Redneck Rampage. It's got these backwoods guys going nuts and chasing each other around with chainsaws."

As if remembering he was at work, the man followed by asking, "How's the room?"

"Fine, nice and clean."

"Yeah, we keep 'em real clean," the man said proudly. "Why, we ain't seen a live roach around here in years."

"Most of the time you won't even know they're there," Joseph responded. "In fact, when you do start seeing them, it means they're out and about because it's getting too crowded."

The gamer shuddered at the thought.

"I hate cockroaches, they give me the creeps in a major way."

"Oh, they're not so bad," Joseph said absently, as he topped off the ice bucket.

"You gotta be kidding, not so bad?"

"Yeah, I know one who's a real good guy."

"What? You better not be bringing any of them around."

"Hey, I was joking, don't worry about it."

"And how long did you say you were staying?"

don't be there when the lights come on

Monday morning arrived with Joseph at his desk, rested and ready for whatever the day might bring. He'd taken Gregory's advice and asked Karen out for Saturday. Sure she wouldn't be available, Joseph was thrilled when she said yes. They went out for dinner and a movie. A simple date, and Joseph was ecstatic, especially when she gave him a lingering kiss goodnight.

"Let's do this again soon, okay?" she'd said.

"Sure, I'd love to."

"There's an antique auto show in town next weekend. Would you like to go with me?"

"Go with you, you mean as in . . ."

"Yeah, another date. You got a problem with a girl asking?"

"Not if it's you, I don't."

"Great, then the deal's sealed. See you Monday morning."

Now it was Monday morning. Karen wasn't in yet, and Mr. Spector hadn't appeared yet either.

The phone rang. Good, Joseph thought, they're in from Chicago and now the show's about to begin.

"Hello?"

"Joseph, Dan Spector here."

"Hi, Mr. Spector, are you downstairs in the lobby?"

Joseph motioned Gregory over to listen in and brought the receiver to desk level so they both could hear.

"No." He laughed abruptly. "I'm out on my ass."

"I don't understand."

"After you left, I went over everything you brought me with my boss, the big cheese, the head of the whole shebang. And, believe me, he wanted heads to roll even worse than me. You should have heard him going on about what he wanted to do to anybody who'd risk dragging the company name through the dirt."

"Thank goodness," Joseph said, breathing a sigh of relief. "I'm glad to hear that."

"Well, don't get too happy. It's not a good ending. After we got all the troops in line and were ready to come in to your place and clean house, the old man happened to mention to his wife what we were up to and she reminded him of a little fact he'd forgotten."

Joseph's heart sank at Dan's tone. He remained silent and waited for the man to continue.

"Turns out that Lindley is his nephew."

"Didn't he know that when he read the report?"

"No. He'd forgotten about it—doesn't see much of his nephew. The problem here is that his sister is a real terror, and seeing as how the company has been in the family a long time, she sits on the board of directors."

"So Lindley stays?"

Dan let out the same abrupt, loud laugh again.

"You bet he stays. He's got my job!"

"You've got to be kidding."

"Wish I was, but it's true. I just called to give you a heads up. Your name's not on the report, but they'll figure it out eventually, so watch your back. If it means anything, I admire what you did. You showed real backbone."

"I've been working on developing a harder shell," Joseph replied quietly.

"Good, because you're going to need it."

Then Mr. Spector was gone.

Joseph looked at Gregory.

"What do I do now?"

Gregory pondered his answer a good, long time. He circled the desk, climbed up and down the pencil sharpener a few times, and even banged his head against the computer keys. Finally he stopped and turned to Joseph with his answer.

"I have no idea."

Joseph had been thinking, too, and a plan was starting to develop.

"Hey, Gregory, just because the company isn't coming in to clean house doesn't mean everything has to stay the same."

"I don't follow you."

"Lindley doesn't know that Smith and Monica are angling to get rid of him, right?"

"Right."

"But, since we know Lindley has this direct connection to the powers that be, what would he do if he found out?"

"Fire Smith and have his uncle get rid of the law firm would be my guess. But how can you let him know without implicating yourself?"

"Watch me."

With Gregory hanging on to a shoelace, Joseph walked over to Lindley's office and knocked.

"Yes, who is it?"

"It's me," Joseph said as he pushed the door open a few inches. "Can I come in for a minute? It's important."

"Come in, have a seat."

"Mr. Lindley," Joseph began, once seated, "this is going to sound strange, but I think Smith and one of the attorneys from the company law firm are going to try forcing you out, with Smith taking your place."

"That's ridiculous," Lindley protested. "They would get away with no such thing."

"I know that, sir, and I also know your uncle is the head of the company that owns this one. Smith doesn't know that, though, and he's out for your job."

"But what could he do to force me out?"

"Nothing, given who your uncle is, but he's got something up his sleeve, and it won't be nice."

"How do I know you're telling the truth?"

"You'll know when the law firm contacts your uncle's people.

Let them know it's coming, then have them tell you when it does."

Lindley thought that over a bit.

"Thanks, Joseph, I'll do that."

Back in the cubicle, Joseph asked Gregory how he thought it had gone.

"Very good, you expressed yourself well. As I've told you, roaches are famous for being able to change directions and move faster than anybody. You, in terms of thinking and act-ing, did something very similar. You saw that the path you'd set for yourself was blocked, so you changed direction and quickly moved to a new destination. In just minutes, you went from having a failed plan to instituting another one just as good."

"Why, thank you. And I assume there is another Rule of the Roach in all this?"

"Yes, but you've already learned it."

"I have?"

"Yes. Lindley is probably talking to his uncle right now. He won't tell him you're the one who clued him in because he wants credit for uncovering the plot. You've already worked it from the head office end with your report, and you had the brains to keep yourself out of that, too."

"So what's the rule?"

"Don't Be There When the Lights Come On."

"Now that makes good sense right off the bat. Because if

somebody goes into their kitchen at night and sees roaches all over the place, you can believe the exterminator will be there in the morning. But if you're smart and know how to make yourself scarce at the right time, you won't become a target."

"Joseph, I couldn't have put it better myself."

Chapter Eighteen

what doesn't exterminate you
only makes you stronger

The sight almost made Joseph feel sorry for him.

"Ah, Joey, I mean Joseph, you got a second?"

Not recognizing the voice, Joseph turned to the hunched form in the doorway and could hardly believe his eyes. It was Harsh, but Harsh as he'd never seen him. There was a brace on his broken nose and huge dark circles around his eyes that made him look like a distressed raccoon. The false front teeth he always wore in place of those he'd lost to a hockey puck in college were missing, and gave him a lisp when he spoke.

"Harsh, how are you?" Joseph asked.

"Hanging in there, I'm hanging in. Thanks for asking."

"Are you coming in to work today?"

"No, and that's the thing, the reason I stopped by. They say I'm only out temporarily, but Smith has already set up shop in my office."

"Did you ask Smith about it?"

"Yeah, I did."

"And?"

Harsh hung his head.

"He told me to get out of his office."

"Well, I don't know what to tell you, Mr. Harshfeld. You and me have had our differences, but I hope that whatever is the matter right now gets cleared up for you before long, I really do."

"You know, Joseph, you're a good guy and I feel bad, real bad, about all the grief I gave you."

"Don't worry about it," Joseph said with a wave of his hand. "The experience helped me develop better motion detectors."

"Huh?" A puzzled look furrowed Harsh's brow, but he plowed on anyway. "What I want to say is that, if you hear anything, or can do anything, or can put in a good word that'll help me get back in, well, I'd be grateful, and I'd make it known, too, I really would."

"Mr. Harshfeld, I believe you."

Joseph stood up and shook the man's hand. Harsh bobbed his head gratefully, then shuffled out of the office.

That encounter had taken place four weeks earlier, and Harsh never did come back. Last Joseph heard, he'd gotten a job driving the Zamboni machine at the rink and worked at the snack bar in between.

Somehow, though, Smith managed to hang on. Lindley moved into Spector's Chicago office and was long gone, but he saw to it that Smith didn't replace him. Instead, Smith was sentenced to Harsh's office—but without the counter or a mandate for abusing the sales staff.

The enforcer of this mandate was Joseph himself, who had been surprised two days after Harsh's appearance to get a phone call at his new apartment from Lindley.

"How are things in Chicago?" Joseph asked after Lindley identified himself.

"It's going well," he replied, "but I'll tell you, I never realized my uncle would be so tough to work for."

"He riding herd on you?"

"Riding herd? He makes Harsh at his worst look like a meek little lamb. I've never worked so hard in my life—and I've only been here a couple days. And get this, my uncle says he's taking it easy on me while I get up to speed."

"Sounds like you're going to be busy."

"Busy isn't the word for it. You know that saying about being careful what you wish for?"

"You mean the one that ends by saying you might get it?"

"Now I know what it means."

Joseph had no reply for that, and after a break in the conversation Mr. Lindley continued.

"I haven't forgotten what you did for me, Joseph, even though I might come to regret being here. So, to show my gratitude, I'm giving you my old job."

"This comes as a total surprise, Mr. Lindley."

"You earned it. The last couple weeks you've shown yourself to be made of much better stuff than I gave you credit for. The job comes with one condition, though."

"What's that?"

"I'm putting Smith in Harsh's old job. And I want you to keep him on a short leash—a choke collar even."

Joseph laughed and replied, "Mr. Lindley, that will be a pleasure."

And it was.

Joseph knew within minutes when the promotion became official. Not by any official communication, but by Smith himself, who was waiting for him by the elevator the morning after his conversation with Lindley.

"Joseph, could I have a word with you?"

"What's up?" Joseph asked. He'd been out with Karen again the night before and was in a wonderful mood.

"I heard the news, that you got Lindley's job. Congratulations, I know you'll be terrific."

"Why thanks, Smith," and Joseph turned to press the elevator button.

"Another thing, if I could."

Joseph turned back toward him. There was something different about Smith this morning. Not just that he was kissing up to him; Joseph had seen him in the same posture with others many times before. No, he looked different somehow.

Smith jerked his head to one side and Joseph knew. The long bangs that, for some unfathomable reason, Smith had maintained so carefully, even though they made him look like a bad 80's New Wave songwriter, were gone. And so was the gel that stank so badly. His hair was clipped short and crisp, with just a hint of mousse in it. And wasn't he dressed like a lawyer, too, at least one of the young up-and-comers from Monica's firm?

"Go ahead, Smith, let's hear it."

"About me and Monica, I . . ."

For once Smith couldn't think of anything to say and just

stood there, with his upraised palms in front of him like he was begging for spare change.

"Don't worry about it. You two are perfect for each other."

A visibly relieved Smith thanked him for his kindness and understanding.

"Come to think of it, Smith, there were a couple of things I wanted to talk to you about."

"Yes?"

"The call-counting machines are toast. And the sales staff, and everybody else who works here, are to be treated with respect."

"But I don't—"

Joseph cut him off with an upraised hand.

"Furthermore, I'm going to be keeping track of your performance. Every person you supervise will be filling out weekly evaluation sheets on you."

"But how can I do my job when they can get back at me like that?"

"What it is, Smith, is reality. And if you don't comply, you're going to have to leave. Is that clear?"

"Yes sir, Mr. Goodrich."

Being in charge was fun, but Joseph was anxious to try different things and go new places. At the invitation of Mr. Moses, he spent a few days in Palm Coast, Florida, and fell in love with it. After a lifetime spent in the frigid, cloudy Northeast, he was more than ready for a change. What puzzled him was why it had taken so long.

Mr. Moses had Karen down on a separate occasion and she

accepted a position as director of marketing and advertising, a nice complement to Joseph's title of director of sales. They were going to live in separate places, for now.

And then the day he'd longed for finally arrived. The moving truck with his and Karen's stuff had already left to take its cargo to their respective apartments. Karen was off visiting her parents and would be in Florida the following week.

Which left Joseph and Gregory.

"Hey, gramps, you ready to go? I'm almost done loading the car."

Slowly, Gregory made his way to the laptop computer he would be traveling in. He was almost seven months old now, ancient for his species of cockroach, and the days were taking their toll. His hearing was okay, but he no longer ran or hopped around like he had just a month earlier.

"Hold your horses, I'm all set to go."

"Gregory, are you sure this is going to be okay?" Joseph asked, motioning to the laptop.

"Sure, us roaches travel all over the country this way. Having a bug in your computer is not just an expression, you know."

"But why not sit up front with me?"

"Joseph, cockroaches were not made for the light of day, especially old ones like me. I just need a safe, warm spot where nobody can see me, that's all."

"After all you've done for me, it seems that you deserve a lot more than that."

"You're doing plenty in return. What with the kids and grandkids and great-grandkids all grown, and my mate, sadly, not lasting as long as I have, Florida is the perfect place for me to wind down."

"You sure?"

"Oh yes, I'll be fine, even if the ride gets bumpy. In fact, that brings me to the final Rule of the Roach."

Joseph snapped his fingers and said, "That's right, I'd forgotten that we left off at number nine."

"Well, I'd better give you number ten before I get any older and forget: What Does Not Exterminate You Only Makes You Stronger."